Transforming Grief:
From Tragedy Emerges Hope

Gavin Perrett

Grosvenor House
Publishing Limited

The right of Gavin Perrett to be identified as the author of this
work has been asserted in accordance with Section 78
of the Copyright, Designs and Patents Act 1988

The book cover is copyright to Gavin Perrett

This book is published by
Grosvenor House Publishing Ltd
Link House
140 The Broadway, Tolworth, Surrey, KT6 7HT.
www.grosvenorhousepublishing.co.uk

A CIP record for this book
is available from the British Library

ISBN 978-1-83975-791-4

Transforming Grief: From Tragedy Emerges Hope

Dedication

This book is dedicated to the memory of my dearly beloved Mother and Father: Christine Dympna Perrett and Brian Clifford Perrett. My love for you both will last for eternity. Thank you for your dedication, belief, kindness, and generosity, which continues to inspire, motivate, and sustain me.

Acknowledgements

I would like to thank the following people for their support and inspiration in helping me to bring this book out of my head and onto paper. To my brother Conal Perrett, thanks to you and your wonderful family for being a constant shining light even during the darkest times. My husband Ian Beaird, thank you for embracing Mum and Dad's love and for speaking about them to me each and every day. My friend and business partner David Liddle, thank you for sharing my personal development journey with me. Thanks to Dan Reed for your ongoing enthusiastic encouragement of my creativity.

And finally, I wish to thank my personal development community for generally being a good influence on me. To Gina Gardiner, I thank you for introducing me to Neurolinguistic Programming. To Ian McDermott, Professor Patricia Riddell, Pamela Richarde, Emma McNally, Robert Dilts, and Tim Hallbom, I thank you for training me and inspiring me to become such a passionate coach.

Introduction

Grief is a sufficiently complex entity on its own without having its fans flamed by a litany of dramatic side stories. In 2020, that is precisely what happened to me. I lost both of my parents to Covid-19 three weeks apart, during a period of international lockdown away from family and friends, whilst continuing to run multiple businesses. It was absolutely crazy and complete mayhem, looking back on it now. How did I get through it? How did I survive? How did I recover, and how did I grow?

Traumatic Grief in complex circumstances is incredibly difficult to navigate. I would like to acknowledge that in the first instance. It is made trickier by virtue of the fact that no two people experience grief in the same way; sure, there are patterns which are reasonably predictable, but the order in which they surface varies wildly from person to person.

What I can supply in this book is empathy by the bucketload. I will take you on a journey deep into my soul, exposing my innermost vulnerability. By baring my soul to you in this way, I open the gates to a harsh reality which I feel is necessary to manage expectations. The brutality of this approach will be balanced by a story of power and hope; how I emerged from the depths of hell to stand tall in a chamber of inner strength and resilience.

My story will then be supported by a series of practical tips that I used to help me get through the darkest days, and strategies that instilled a sense of peace when it felt like the whole world around me was going mad. I will also share how I reframed my sense of perspective to grow my businesses during the most aggressive recession that the world has seen in years, whilst simultaneously battling my grief.

I combine my personal experience of grief with my experience and expertise as a coach to produce this book, which is designed to inspire hope and empower those who have also experienced tragic loss. It can also be used as a handbook to help those who have suffered loss in other ways, such as relationship break-ups, redundancy, financial loss, and bankruptcy, to name a few.

I felt compelled to write this book, not only to share a profoundly personal story, but also to outline how limiting beliefs and fear can be replaced with a sense of energy and empowerment that can be harnessed to positively transform your life forever.

I am genuinely excited about the prospect of inspiring my readers to overcome adversity to become the best version of themselves.

'What we once enjoyed and deeply loved we can never lose, for all that we love deeply becomes part of us.'

Helen Keller

'They that love beyond the world cannot be separated by it. Death cannot kill what never dies.'

William Penn

'Love is really the only thing we can possess, keep with us, and take with us.'

Elisabeth Kubler-Ross

Chapter 1

My Childhood & Family History

To fully understand the nature and dynamics of my family, and thereby appreciate the intensity of the grief that followed, I am going to offer an insight into my childhood. Hopefully, a little background and context will be helpful.

My father, Brian Clifford Perrett, was born in Sliema in Malta on the 16th February, 1940. My mother, Christine Dympna Holland (later known as Debbie), was born in Kilchreest, County Galway in Ireland, on the 13th December, 1942. They both arrived in England from their respective countries in the 1950s as teenagers, demonstrating immense courage as they left home to seek out opportunities in a new and unfamiliar territory. What is interesting is that I have been aware of this fact for many years, however it is only now that they are both gone that I sit here in awe of their bravery. I regret not asking them both what it was like to leave home at the age of 15 and 17 respectively, either alone and certainly without their parents, to cultivate a new life in a foreign country. I would like to feel that they both saw it as an adventure, and hope that they weren't too afraid or lonely. I suspect in reality it was a bit of both, largely due to the way that they brought up my brother and me; fiercely protective over us, whilst encouraging us to travel and experience different cultures.

Dad joined the British Army and, having spent time in Yorkshire, Scotland, and Germany, he finally settled down and bought a house in Southall in Middlesex. Mum, meanwhile, trained to become a dispensing chemist, and took up residence in Crouch End. For many years I was convinced that my parents met in the Catholic Social Club after mass one Sunday; however, in reality they met in a nightclub in the West End of London. Mum was enjoying a night out with her cousin when Dad pitched up at the bar and asked Valerie what Mum was likely to want to drink. A gin and tonic followed, and six months later Mum and Dad tied the knot on October 21st, 1967.

My brother Conal was born on November 21st, 1971, and soon afterwards they moved to Brentwood in Essex. By this time, Dad had left the Army and embarked upon a career in telecommunications, which saw him commute to Mayfair in the first instance and then settle in the City near St Paul's Cathedral, where he would remain working for Mitsubishi Corporation until his retirement in the year 2000. Mum stopped work to raise her family and manage the house – a lovely, detached house with a big garden, in a friendly neighbourhood not far from a country park.

I was born on July 1st, 1974, at Harold Wood Hospital. That was it for Mum and Dad – two boys! Conal and I would plead with our parents (in vain) to have one more child, as I think we both wanted to have a little sister. With the benefit of hindsight, I think that it was a blessing we didn't. I can only begin to imagine how traumatising it would be to have Conal and me as older brothers, purely from a protectiveness perspective.

Our childhood was punctuated with happy memories that had their foundation in our parents' unconditional love and commitment to their two boys. Every summer we would visit

Ireland on holiday, and stay there for three weeks. We would travel by car, either to Liverpool or Holyhead, and get the ferry across to either Howth Harbour or Dun Laoghaire in Dublin. We would then spend a few days each with Mum's sister Lucy, her husband Stan, and our cousins Sian and Tara. and then on to Mum's brother Mike and his wife Mary, who lived – and still do live – in Templeogue. Our annual family odyssey then continued with a five-hour car journey, meandering through the Irish mainland, heading west to County Galway. After a pitstop in Maynooth to visit Mum's other brother Peter and his family, we would eventually arrive to the lovingly open arms of our wonderful grandparents.

Annie and Martin Holland lived in a modest bungalow in a village called Kilchreest, which is situated between Loughrea and Gort. Before they retired, they were farmers, and all four of their children were born and raised in that bungalow. They were fortunate to live in a beautiful, secluded part of Galway's stunning farmland. Rolling hills and historic forts greeted us upon arrival, and the only sound that you could hear would be the distant murmur of a tractor's engine or the crows that nested in the very tall trees on our neighbour's land a few hundred metres down the road.

We would spend three weeks each summer in Ireland, and the two-week spell in Galway would offer us an opportunity to spend time with the many second cousins that lived nearby. Our grandparents' house was a good base from which we could explore, taking in Galway City itself, the beautiful fishing village of Kinvara, and of course, the Wild Atlantic Way. Touring the west coast of Ireland is something that I will never tire of, and to this day I look forward to visiting the Cliffs of Moher in all of their glory.

We visited Malta less often, probably due to the expense of flying a family of four, which in the late 1970s and early to mid-1980s I imagine was reasonably prohibitive. I think that we went there on two occasions during our childhood, however I have been lucky enough to return several times as an adult. Once again, relatives were in abundance in Malta just like in Ireland, and this is one of the wonderful aspects of coming from such a large extended family. I think that Conal and I probably had the best of both worlds, in that we enjoyed the intimacy of our smaller immediate family whilst enjoying the benefits of uncles, aunties, and cousins, whose numbers probably ran into the low hundreds.

Back home in Brentwood, school and church became the combined epicentre of our childhood experience. Both Conal and I attended St Helen's Infant and then Junior School in Brentwood, before attending The Campion School in Hornchurch for the secondary school phase of our education. The common denominator here was the fact that they were Catholic schools, underpinned by a close connection to St Helen's Cathedral which was also in Brentwood. Further strengthening those ties were my contribution as a chorister and an altar server for the church, which on many occasions meant that I attended two mass services per Sunday. I enjoyed being part of that community, and many of my school friends also participated, which was nice for us all and our parents.

Mum and Dad created this environment for us, purely to give us the best possible start in life. They appreciated and understood that if you surround your children with love and likeminded people, who share similar values in a supportive community, then hopefully there's a foundation upon which to build a good life. Our parents were never pushy, and always gave us the freedom to make decisions for ourselves, albeit guided and encouraged by them. All they wanted for us was to be happy and to try our best at whatever we applied ourselves to.

My childhood was punctuated by poor health. I suffer with Coeliac Disease, and sadly it remained undiagnosed until the age of ten; this was despite me suffering with the condition from birth. My mother, however, saw this as a challenge, and despite the inconvenience of having to introduce gluten-free cooking (a necessity for those with Coeliac Disease), she 'took the bull by the horns' and became proficient in mastering gluten-free cookery. This was no mean feat in 1984, when gluten-free food substitutes enjoyed as much flavour and substance as a cardboard box that had been left out in the rain for a few days.

Ultimately their focus, drive, and ambition were anchored to their commitment to their two boys. Our mother, in particular, took her role intensely seriously when it came to protecting us. In reality we didn't need much protection, living in a pleasant suburb and embraced in a safe community within the Catholic school and church arena. That said, Mum had a razor-sharp focus when it came to standing up for Conal and me. Her antennae were always on alert, ready to detect any undue criticism, or behaviour towards us that was less than kind. Sometimes our mother's intervention was welcome, but on other occasions it was excruciatingly embarrassing. And I know that both Conal and I will recall a number of events where we both wanted to curl up and die following Mum's Amazonian approach to defending her sons. Other children, their parents, and teachers were included in various line-ups over the years.

Dad was less belligerent in his approach to parenthood, and simply wanted to know who we were hanging out with, to make sure that they didn't lead us astray. One solid memory of the sacrifices that Dad made for us was his attention to detail with saving money. From the age of 15 onwards my favourite pastime, which has lasted the distance until today, was my love of live music. Almost on a weekly basis whilst in sixth form, I would trek up to London on the train with my good friends John, David, and James, and head for The Astoria, The Forum, Brixton Academy, or Wembley Arena, to see the likes of AC/DC, Bon Jovi, Van Halen, David Lee Roth, Extreme, and Dan Reed Network. Dad would sacrifice his lunch break once per week to head directly to the venue in question to purchase the tickets for the four of us, in order to save the £2.50 booking fee per ticket that would have been levied had they been booked over the phone by credit card. Looking back now, I'm mortified that I let him do that, but at the tender age of 16 I simply accepted that this was the sort of kind action that Dad wouldn't think twice about doing simply to help his son save money.

Neither Mum nor Dad ever received any financial help from their parents when they were younger, simply because there was no money to give. Despite not earning high salaries themselves, they were determined to help us both save money where possible, and to shield us from the difficulties that they experienced when they were young. In fact, the best example of this was during the recession of 1989-1981. I had no idea whatsoever that there was anything challenging going on with the economy – not a clue! The only memory that I can reference was after passing my driving test in 1991, Mum making sure that I didn't go out driving too much due to the cost of petrol.

Both Conal and I graduated from The Campion School and progressed to higher education. Conal studied medicine at Bristol University, and a few years later I set off to University College London to read Classics. Thankfully, this was back in the day before tuition fees had been introduced; however, I know putting two children through university (simultaneously for a couple of years) was challenging for our parents financially. Again, we were never exposed to those challenges, and it's only with the benefit of hindsight that I have an awareness of this. It was a tremendous source of pride to Mum and Dad that both of their sons achieved academic success at university, particularly given their own humble backgrounds. They were, in fact, overjoyed and so happy to know that we had achieved an early milestone that would hopefully see us engineering a stable pathway to financial security and fulfilment. I guess that was their main concern; first and foremost, not struggling in any way, taking pride in whatever we decided to do, and giving it our best shot.

We both graduated from our respective universities in 1996, and entered the next journey of our lives, stepping into adulthood in earnest, and embracing – albeit tentatively – the responsibility that accompanies that life milestone. We both enjoyed our time at Bristol and London respectively, and despite loving our home life with Mum and Dad, fully embraced the experience of living away from home, making new friends and connections, many of whom we are still in touch with today.

Chapter 2

Our Parents' Love and Support throughout adulthood

Having graduated from university, I naively thought that life was going to be more straightforward now that I was a big boy heading into the world of business, making my own decisions, and having the freedom to be my own boss. I could not have been more wrong; it's actually very amusing looking back now at how naive I was at the age of 22. I wouldn't say that I was arrogant at all back then, but I certainly thought that my strongly held opinions and beliefs were right, and I was fully confident that they would stand up to scrutiny. More of that later…

I didn't have a clue what I wanted to do after I left UCL. I knew that I didn't want to become an academic or take the traditional route into the 'City', working for an investment bank. I did in fact want to work within the music industry, not because I actually wanted to work within that industry but more so that I could work with likeminded people who loved and appreciated great music. My first dalliance into the music business manifested itself in September 1996 with a one-month spell doing work experience for an independent record label. I must have written to every record company in London to try and get some form of experience, and I am fairly sure that this firm was the only one to respond. As it happens, they were a decent player in the independent sector and signed some big names, or more accurately, some names that became big. Unfortunately, it didn't go anywhere, and I ended up stuffing promotional CDs into Jiffy bags each day, being promised by a manager that my expenses would get covered, which of course never materialised. I was also quite disappointed by how disingenuous some of the staff were to each other. Lots of smiles, airs and graces, with sly comments as soon as people were out of earshot. I decided that it wasn't for me, put it down to experience, and moved on.

God only knows what I would be like as a parent! I can't imagine for a moment that I would have hidden my true feelings and opinions as diplomatically as my parents did in relation to the quality of some of my early decision making. Looking back now, I don't have any significant regrets about the decisions that I made when I was young, simply because I take a philosophical approach to life, and trust that each episode – regardless of the quality of the experience – was instrumental in me becoming the person that I am today. I do, however, believe that I was incredibly naive when I was the tender age of 22, and I wouldn't at all be surprised if my visualisation of Mum and Dad with their heads in their hands, despondent that I appeared to be making a series of backward steps, was indeed more than a comedic fantasy.

Unfortunately for them, my aspirations of making my mark in the music industry didn't quite finish there. There was one final attempt on my part that followed soon after the record company incident, that would then put my aspirations into hibernation until many years later. I got it into my head that I could come in handy for Sharon and Ozzy Osbourne; a facilitator, fixer, and executive assistant, all rolled into one. How hard could it be? I spent a few days brushing up on the details of all of the bands that Sharon was managing, posted my CV to her, and then followed up with a phone call to her secretary. To my abject amazement, I received an invitation to visit them for an interview. I told my parents and watched as the blood drained from their faces as they uttered words of encouragement to me. Thankfully for them, the interview was cancelled at short notice, and I never heard from the Osbournes again. I have no idea why, although thankfully there was no social media back then to inspire a harrowing wave of paranoia. In reality, I suspect it had something to do with them heading over to Los Angeles to sort out some Ozzfest-related issues, or at least that is what I have told myself and it feels like a great story, so let's stick with that.

Let us not forget the Japan incident. I have always been a curious soul, and if an organisation was good enough to offer me an interview, I would attend it regardless of whether I intended to take up the position or not. I did not expect to receive a job offer from the good folks at TEFL (Teaching English as a Foreign Language). I did consider it for a few days before concluding that it probably wasn't for me. By this time, Mum and Dad were probably beginning to see the appeal of me moving to the Far East, as this latest hair-brained chapter triggered the latest succession of metaphorical eye rolls. I also applied for a job as a Latin teacher at a private primary school near Hastings that looked like Hogwarts. I got turned down for that job interview after I mistook a phone a call from the Headmaster for a call from Dad, who normally rang at that time of the morning. I was hungover and slipped running out of the shower to answer the phone, and launched into a foul-mouthed tirade at who I thought was my father, only for the creeping reality to dawn upon me that it was in fact a potential future employer. Oh dear...

Whilst all of this was going on, I did actually carve out a decent part-time career as a private tutor. A chance request by one of my former Professors at UCL led to an opportunity to tutor an A Level student with her Latin studies. This was a classic case of me agreeing to doing something, and then figuring out how I was going to fulfil the obligation along the way. Incredibly, it succeeded, and the student achieved her desired grade following my tuition. It quickly dawned on me, though, that there wasn't going to be a huge demand for A Level or GCSE private tuition in Essex where I lived. The previous student had been based in Notting Hill, which was fine, as a one-off comfortably coincided with a trip to London to meet up with friends for drinks afterwards. It wasn't, however, something that was practical on a wider basis. So, I figured that English Literature and Language was going to be an easier route to market local to me in Brentwood, Upminster, Hornchurch, and Romford. Within a matter of weeks, my diary was full each weekday evening and all-day Saturday, with students whose parents had decided that school alone was not going to get their children to achieve their desired grades. I supplemented this enterprise with three shifts per week at my local pub, The Nag's Head. I think I saved more money by not going out rather than the money earned on the shifts, but combined with my tutor earnings, I made a decent wage whilst living at home, which more than paid for my beer money.

My relationship with Mum and Dad was healthy, and they loved having me live at home. We've always sustained our relationship on a level playing field, treating one another more as friends in certain respects than parents and son. I know that they admired my work ethic, and I guess this was an early sign of my attitude towards business, and my intense desire to learn and educate had its genesis in my time as a tutor. Whilst they knew that this period was a temporary stop gap for me, they knew that I was acquiring skills that would serve me well in the future. I didn't consciously know this, but the fact that I was happy to trust my instincts that this was a good thing to do meant that I took value from this episode. Looking back, I know precisely how I have benefited from this period.

And then I stumbled headlong into financial services, completely and utterly by accident. If you'd have told me when I graduated from university that I was going to end up working in financial services, I would have been horrified. It was the antithesis of the vision that I had for my future, and I would have regarded it as 'selling out'. The only reason that I ended up considering this sector was due to me responding to the vaguest of adverts in a copy of the *Evening Standard* that I picked up on the train on the way home from Liverpool Street one evening, following some drinks with university friends.

My naivety resurfaced again at this stage when I accepted the 'job', working as a self-employed financial adviser as a tied agent to an American insurance company. Despite participating in five interviews, the stark reality that I would be working on a commission only basis with no salary eluded me. I probably had an inkling that this was the case, but true to form I buried my head in the sand, and blissfully and optimistically hoped that a form of regular income would magically manifest itself each month. Of course, it didn't!

Once again, however, I have no regrets, as the experience taught me resilience and encouraged strength of character to emerge. Despite never having been in business themselves, Mum and Dad fostered an enthusiastic curiosity with both of our business endeavours. Although business advice *per se* wasn't forthcoming from our parents, inspiration was there from the word go. Maintaining high standards, treating people with respect, and fostering great long-term relationships, were at the forefront of our parents' expectations for both Conal and me.

The recession of 2008 was a deeply troubling period for me. My business suffered as a result of the lack of availability of mortgage lending, and at that time mortgage broking represented 80% of my income. At times during that recession, the outlook for me financially was bleak. Mum and Dad, however, never judged me, despite me making some pretty big mistakes. Looking back now, I think that they respected the fact that I never hid problems from them. I had a tendency to want to share everything that was going on in my life – good, bad, and indifferent – with them. It was difficult, because part of me wanted to shield them from my problems, so that they didn't experience undue worry, anxiety, or concern. I knew, though, that ultimately they would rather know so that they could help me. Any time that I delayed speaking to them about a problem, they subsequently advised that they knew something was wrong and were hoping that I would eventually confide in them. I always did, eventually, and always felt a palpable sense of relief.

Conal and I have always been so fortunate that our parents supported our personal relationships. When I came out as gay to Mum and Dad at the age of 25 (having come out to my friends at the age of 22), their only concern was that I would be happy. Nothing else mattered to them, and despite having limited experience of knowing many people who were gay, they never made me feel uncomfortable or awkward.

Conal married Miranda in 2008, and in 2010 my niece Isabel was born, with Georgia following in 2013. I met Ian in 2009, and we were married in 2013. Our parents loved our partners dearly and, of course, their granddaughters, who were their pride and joy. As our families expanded, Mum and Dad's focus and attention expanded, and it gave them a new lease of life at a time when Mum's health was steadily becoming more challenging.

I will close this chapter by thanking an old colleague of mine for some sage advice that he gave me that, thankfully, I acted upon. I used to work with a chap called Clint. He lost his dad as a child, and then his mother whilst he was still only in his thirties. We worked quite closely together, and he could see how close I was to my parents. One day out of the blue, he advised me to spontaneously and without any reason book a weekend break for Mum and Dad. I didn't appreciate at the time why he suggested that, but I was still quite young and impressionable back then, and of course it was a lovely thing to do, so why not? I subsequently paid for my parents to visit Prague for a weekend break. That, I think, was in 2003. I then in 2006 paid for them to accompany me to New York for a long weekend. They enjoyed both trips immensely, but the one memory that will stay with me forever is the look of awe, joy, and amazement on my parents' faces when they looked out of the limousine window as we approached Manhattan, and witnessed the majestic skyline. This is one of the happiest moments of my life, seeing them both so excited with an almost childlike curiosity. I am so grateful for this memory – thank you, Clint!

Chapter 3

Living with Illness & Disability

Some people, as they age, for some reason don't seem to act or behave older. Both of my parents adopted a youthful attitude towards life, and I never really noticed them ageing. Their curious and positive outlook on life kept them fresh, both in their physical realities and also in my mind. They were always busy, either maintaining the family home, helping Conal and me with the maintenance of our homes, assisting with moving house, going on holiday, visiting family and friends; the list goes on...

Arguably, they would have done more and kept busier, but there were a number of health challenges that put the brakes on some of these aspirations. In this chapter, I will outline how Mum and Dad coped and dealt with illness and disability throughout their married lives. The reason I do this is not to court sympathy, and it certainly has no bearing on how they eventually died; it does, however, highlight their dogged determination to persevere in the face of extreme adversity, their stoic acceptance of matters beyond their control, and how they inspired others in similar situations never to give up hope.

Dad had always been fit and healthy. He was rarely sick, and bounced back quickly when he was. If ever he fell ill, it would only ever be something as innocuous as a head cold. I think that his grounding in the Army prepared him well for life, and he maintained strong physical fitness and dexterity throughout his adult life. So, when in 2010 he found a lump in the back of his head, he didn't appear unduly concerned. The only reason that he even mentioned it was because he could feel it every time he lifted his head back, and my mother – who was probably still cutting his hair by that point – had noticed it as she was giving him his monthly trim.

Mum obviously sent him to the doctor, who examined Dad and sent him off for a biopsy. The day that Dad received his biopsy results, I was out socialising with friends in London. Some friends of mine were heading over to live in Portugal for a few years, as part of a work placement. Our group of friends were celebrating a send-off at a bar in Waterloo, I think. I headed back home at around 10pm, at which point I uncharacteristically rang Mum and Dad. It was quite normal for me to call them every day, and sometimes twice a day, but generally not quite that late at night. Dad had played down the lump and told me it was a cyst to stop me from worrying, so I had no reason to anxiously keep checking in with him whilst the biopsy was underway. For some reason, that evening I decided to check in with them. Mum answered the phone to me, and I immediately knew that something was wrong.

There was almost a telepathic sixth sense phenomenon between myself and the people closest to me. When I was a child, I was particularly sensitive to atmosphere, changes in mood, tension, etc – often when nobody else was in the room with me to signpost that there had perhaps been an argument moments before. I can't explain why, but I could sense negative tension before I entered a room or as I made a phone call. And I always had a predisposition to fall ill when a close family member was dying. I remember clearly when my maternal grandfather was dying in Ireland. We knew that he was poorly and slowly deteriorating as a result of Parkinson's Disease and Dementia, however I am fairly confident that we didn't think that he was so close to death. I was ten years of age at the time, and was at church on a Sunday morning. It was, in fact, the Ursuline Convent in Brentwood which was acting as a *de facto* Cathedral whilst the Cathedral itself was being renovated. I was a choirboy and performing at the Sunday morning service. I rapidly started to feel unwell, but I persevered, never wanting to cause a fuss. Obviously, this was stupid of me – I was a little boy in intense pain, and I should have discreetly removed myself from the situation, sought out my parents, and let them take me home.

Instead, my eyes were transfixed on my father. He was stood on the opposite side of the church with Mum. His eyes caught my gaze, and I could see tears running down his face. He was palpably upset, but he just carried on and said nothing to anybody. One of my regrets before Dad died was that I never spoke to him about this episode afterwards, either immediately or years later in adulthood. I am utterly convinced that he knew that Grandpa was dying, not consciously but subconsciously. Somehow the reality of what was happening over in Ireland was manifesting itself in Dad's heart and in my body. My pain came from nowhere, and coincided with Dad's experience. Grandpa wasn't even my dad's father; he was Mum's father. But Dad loved him as if he was his father, and the feeling was reciprocated. Dad knew how much Mum loved Grandpa, and it would have devastated him to have an awareness of how much grief she was about to encounter.

Just thinking about this episode now makes me yearn to have spoken with both Mum and Dad about their own experiences of grief. Both grandfathers died when I was ten, and both grandmothers when I was in my twenties and thirties. As a child, I wouldn't have had an awareness of how I could have helped them, but I did as an adult, and I hope I helped them both in some small way. I can't prove that this episode carries anything more than coincidental significance, however my intuition suggests otherwise, and this is something that has served me well over the years.

So, back to the phone call in 2010. As soon as Mum answered the phone that night, I knew that something was wrong – and quite seriously wrong. She tried to fob me off and encourage me to call back in the morning to discuss 'it' properly, but I was having none of it and wanted to know there and then what was going on. Mum was crying hysterically, so Dad calmly took the phone and explained that he had been diagnosed with a low-grade lymphoma. In the grand scheme of things, and with the benefit of hindsight, this wasn't actually too big a deal. At the age of 70, and with a low-grade cancer, the chance of it spreading – and indeed spreading quickly – was relatively remote. The doctors decided quite sensibly that Dad, who was otherwise fit and healthy, did not need his body blasted with chemotherapy or radiotherapy. He simply had to visit Bart's Hospital Oncology department every three months for a physical examination and a blood test. These examinations would continue for the rest of his life, stretching out to every six and then 12 months, as he approached the age of 80.

At the time, though, I was petrified, as my mind and imagination darted off in a million different directions trying to work out the probability of all of the various outcomes. Thankfully, a measured conversation with Conal the next day helped me to put the situation into a sense of perspective. I was still very worried, but aware that at this stage at least it was far from being any form of death sentence. Dad was lucky; after a few years, we all forgot that he had cancer, and he might as well not have had it. Thank God, as our biggest fear as a family was always how Mum and Dad would cope if anything happened to him. Mum's independent mobility had been compromised for about five years by this point, and the situation was not going to improve. As far as latent fears were concerned, this one was about as acute as you could get.

Mum, on the other hand, collected maladies and battled various health conditions throughout her life, and for as long as I can remember. When I was a child, I tend to remember her having a lot of physiotherapy for painful shoulders and battling fatigue. The reality was that she was plagued with mixed connective tissue diseases from adolescence onwards. As a family, we have always had our suspicions about the dangers of farmers' kids playing near sheep dips that were awash with toxic chemicals, and the lasting effects that could have had on anyone working or playing either directly in the sheep dip or nearby. We simply don't know if there is any relevance here, but it's certainly been a discussion point over the years.

I'll attempt to list all of Mum's illnesses: Rheumatism, arthritis, Lupus, Scleroderma, Sjogren's Syndrome, Myxoedema, and Raynaud's Syndrome. Not all at the same time, I hasten to add, however they were interspersed with various surgical procedures, including gall bladder removal, numerous spinal surgeries (including the partial reconstruction of Mum's spinal cage with titanium), two hip replacement operations, and various bone graft procedures. After a while I started calling Mum 'Darth Vader', as she was rapidly becoming more machine than man. It's okay, Mum had a great sense of humour when it came to her health, and it's probably what kept her going.

For all of the above, we as a family never really worried about any potential threat to her life. With each operation and surgical procedure, the heaviest concern would have been surviving the anaesthetic, purely as a numbers' game, and the increased risk purely by virtue of volume of procedures.

Throughout her life Mum's challenges were predominantly centred around mobility and pain management. I am pretty sure that she had the highest pain threshold of anyone that I have ever met or known.

Mum's steely determination to keep going, and an inner resilience that shielded her from desperation, ensured that she never ever gave up. In fact, one of her favourite words was 'hope'. 'I'll never give up hope, Gav,' she'd say, and I truly believe that it was this hope that gave her the strength to continue. I'm fairly sure that this hope stemmed from her Catholic faith, and whilst she wasn't overtly religious, she had sufficient purchase in the framework of faith, community, and spirit, to recognise a higher purpose and be comfortable directing her attention in that direction.

Conal, Ian, and I regularly reflect with kind and fond humour on Mum's insistence that she would start driving again when she was well into her seventies. This was following two hip replacement operations and spinal reconstruction surgery. Dad would have to leave the room whenever Mum started talking about her driving ambitions; it was so funny! We could all imagine poor old Mum bunny-hopping along in the driving instructor's car as she valiantly fought to reclaim her driving licence (she never lost her licence; I am simply referring to the over-70s having to resit their driving test). Whilst Conal, Ian, and I found this really funny, Dad's sense of humour was stifled with fear of this dream emerging into some form of horrific reality. And, of course, it never did happen, which is fine because Mum was happy enough to cling onto the hope that it would some day, and she never really let go of that. None of us, however, was stupid or insensitive enough to rain on her parade.

Ever since I can remember as a very young child, Mum battled with poor health. I didn't know any different, and thought that this was normal. I can recall parents of my friends asking me (out of courtesy) how Mum was; I assumed that they automatically had an awareness of her full medical history and were making enquiries about the latest updates of Mum's condition. Looking back now, and somewhat embarrassingly, I can see that they were making polite small talk. Unfortunately for them, they would then receive a ten-minute long (probably felt longer for them) detailed account and synopsis of Mum's various hospital and doctors' appointments. I would have been about nine years old at the time, and I don't think I ever told Mum. She would have been horrified at the time, but would have found it funny now.

As I said earlier, none of these health challenges ever felt life-threatening. Life-limiting, certainly. We, as a family, were used to Mum's life-changing conditions, and adapted accordingly. We were never really concerned about her losing her life, but more upset and worried about how much pain she was in, and feeling helpless to do anything to help her. This makes what happened later so much more difficult to comprehend.

Chapter 4

2018: Back living with Mum & Dad

As I cast my mind back to February 2018, I am smiling; smiling as I recall one of the happiest periods of my life. Ian and I had spent the previous six years enjoying a slightly nomadic lifestyle living in some of Essex's most pleasant villages (Stock & Ingatestone), and then in the New Year of 2018 we decided to move a little further out into North Essex. We found a charming house in Braintree that we fell in love with and put an offer in, which was promptly accepted.

There was, however, a gap of three months between us leaving our house in Ingatestone and moving into our new house in Braintree. This briefly left us with a dilemma about where we were going to live and store all of our stuff during a period which was shorter than most tenancy agreements. The dilemma was indeed short-lived, as we were invited to live with Mum and Dad during this window, and of course we gracefully accepted their kind offer.

For me, this was a no-brainer, but I was slightly tentative about how Ian would feel about living with his in-laws. After all, this was the house that I was born and brought up in, and I knew every inch of the property back to front and blindfolded. It was remarkably easy for me to move back there and immediately feel comfortable. Put it this way, ever since I had moved out of that house in my twenties, I had referred to wherever I lived at the time as 'home'. But I always referred to Mum and Dad's house as 'home'.

I needn't have been worried about Ian, though, as he settled in well and made himself at home. Ian, in particular, I feel benefitted from this stay, as he got to know and love Mum and Dad even more than he did before. I know for a fact that they felt the same way as him. This made my heart leap with joy, and made me feel like my life was complete. Looking back and reflecting now, it feels like it was meant to be, almost as if this was one final chance for us all to bond intensely and enjoy each other's company. I'm aware of how fatalistic this sounds, but with the benefit of hindsight it is difficult to avoid feeling this way.

Some of our friends thought that we were stark raving mad. There was me at the age of 43 moving back in with my parents, along with my 36-year-old husband. A few eyebrows were raised when I optimistically referenced our plan to our friends; not in a mean-spirited way, but out of genuine concern. I think perhaps that some of them were concerned for Ian, not being as familiar with the house and my parents as I was, but also given their knowledge of me and my idiosyncratic personality. Allow me to explain! I am a creature of habit; I thrive upon routine, structure, and having all of my metaphorical 'ducks in a row'. I operate and work very well in such an environment, but if I am feeling tired and unresourceful, then external influences which tamper with some of the more linear aspects of my personality can be met with a little resistance. Read into that what you will...

Whilst the summary above is indeed accurate, I also am by nature an optimist who seeks out the good in any situation. Whilst routine is a comfort to me, if change is required to facilitate an outcome that I am devoted to, I can flex with ease.

Had I not had such a great relationship with my parents, I would have flexed, as this was a means to an end. However, it was much more than that; it was one of the most magical and wonderful experiences of my life, and I loved every minute of it. Having Ian spend so much time with Mum and Dad afforded the opportunity to reminisce and share stories about our family from years ago. Ian (thankfully) has a natural curiosity, so he embraced these stories warmly.

In reality, we were hardly there during the day. I was at work in my office in Chelmsford each day, and Ian was sporadically driving to and from Heathrow Airport, as at the time he was working for British Airways. The evenings and weekends were when we spent the most time together. I dread to think how much weight we put on during that three-month window, as Mum and Dad fed us as if we were expecting a famine. Neither of us were used to a three-course meal every evening, but that is exactly what we got. I can still hear my dad shuffling into the lounge with some late evening snacks (after the three-course meal) and cups of tea (or was it glasses of wine?) just in case we'd become peckish.

We made the most of it whilst we were there, embracing The Nags Head pub a short walk away as our 'local', and I took to utilising the nearby country park as a training ground for the forthcoming half marathon that I was participating in.

I like to think that Mum and Dad derived as much enjoyment from this period as Ian and I did. I am sure that they did, and as such I can reflect and look back upon this chapter with joy, gratitude, and a sense of fulfilment. We were so lucky to have this opportunity just two years before they died. This is one of the reasons that I can look back without any real regrets. If I cast my mind back on my whole life, it is one that is filled with an abundance of wonderful memories of our parents. We never fell out, said anything to each other that we regretted later, and had no periods where we didn't speak to one another. Sure, we bickered like every family does, but that was it.

It's so important to be able to measure a relationship with precious chunks of time that have been spent together. Experiences, memories, conversations, shared meals, and holidays, all symbolise how we feel about our loved ones. And the great thing about this is that nobody and nothing can ever take this away, and that is empowering if you allow it to be so.

Chapter 5

2020: Mum

Mum's health had challenged her as far back as I can remember, to the extent where I was simply used to her not being in full health. Notice how I didn't refer to her as being ill; this is deliberate. Whilst Mum battled poor health, I never regarded her as ill. Because we were as family so used to Mum's reality, it normalised it for us, and I guess we accepted it as just the way it was for her.

Mum's calendar was littered with appointments for the GP and hospital consultants, either locally in Essex or in London. These appointments were supported by visits to physiotherapists, chiropodists, pain relief specialists, and many, many more. Then, of course, there were the various operations and surgical procedures that punctuated Mum's timeline. Gallstones, shoulder surgery, gall bladder removal, bone grafts, multiple spinal surgeries, and hip replacement procedures. Her poor body had been ravaged by surgery to the extent where you may recall from an earlier chapter that I playfully referred to her as 'Darth Vader – more machine than man'.

Despite all of this, we never as a family really worried about her life being in danger. All of our concerns were focused on her rehabilitation and the practicalities of getting her back on her feet again. The first time that I experienced genuine concern that her life might have started to become in jeopardy was in December 2017. She ended up in hospital with sepsis, and this condition quite understandably terrified her. She wasn't remotely bothered at the prospect of having a titanium cage being erected with her spinal frame (as she had a few years prior), but sepsis really, really scared her. I remember visiting her in hospital and I could see that she was worried; this, in turn, meant that I was also starting to get a little scared, and I did wonder whether we might lose her. There was certainly an element of me not worrying about Mum too much, as long as she wasn't too worried about herself. It was almost like Mum had an intuition about her health, and looking back now, I think that I subconsciously was in tune with her intuition and used it as a barometer to adjust the level of concern that I had at any given moment. I think perhaps it was my way of preserving my energy levels, and in turn a form of anxiety management. Thankfully, her steely resilience shone through once again and she recovered, home in time for Christmas.

Mum's health remained steady for the next two years, but slowly began to deteriorate towards the second half of 2019. This time, it was her circulation (or lack of thereof) that presented significant danger. Both of her legs and feet had become increasingly swollen over an extended period of time. They had also become discoloured, gradually turning a deep shade of purple. This resulted in Mum experiencing excruciating pain, and made it even more difficult for her to walk. Ever since the series of hip and spine operations a decade before, she had relied to one extent or another on either crutches or a zimmer frame. At this point, even with the aid of these support devices, she struggled to walk and would take a very long time to travel even the shortest distance.

One memory that stands out in particular during this period was Mum's 77th birthday on 13th December, 2019. Her mobility was severely restricted by that point, but the family decided to be a little courageous and attempt a slightly different birthday altogether. My niece Isabel was performing in *The Nutcracker*, which was being shown at a West End theatre. We were all very keen to see her performance, and we arranged to meet up there along with members of my sister-in-law Miranda's family. My brother and his family live in central London, whilst I live in Essex, as did my parents.

It was my responsibility that day to chaperone Mum and Dad safely between their home in Brentwood and the theatre in the West End (and back again). Given Mum's disability, I was fully aware in advance that the journey had potential to evolve into a challenge of mythological proportions – an odyssey of sorts! Allowing plenty of time, we decided to navigate the journey via the public transport system, using the trains and underground system, with Dad and I ferrying Mum in her wheelchair, and carefully selecting the tube stations that had the benefit of wheelchair access lifts. I think in the end we made it to Westminster tube station before 'jumping in a cab' to the theatre. The journey was not at all easy. In fact, I think it would have been easier to have carried Mum on a sedan chair rather than her tortuous wheelchair. Even without the luxury of state elephants and six virgins scattering rose petals to clear a path before us, it probably would have been a lot easier.

The return journey was even more challenging. This time, we had to endure the additional handicap of London Friday evening rush hour on the underground. I thought that we had planned our journey well, but for reasons that I cannot remember now we opted to take the circle line back to Liverpool Street. On the way back this was a problem, because the train arrives at a platform on the other side of a set of bridge steps. Obviously (now at least), we could have taken the longer route in the other direction and arrived on a nearer platform without the need to ascend and descend any steps. It is easy to assess these things in retrospect, with the benefit of hindsight.

It must have taken poor Mum twenty minutes to negotiate the steps, supported by Dad and me. It didn't help that a young lady commuter tutted as my mother's slow place halfway across the bridge presumably delayed her journey to her ongoing destination by a mere five seconds. Now, as you will see from the forthcoming chapter on anger, I am by nature a calm, peaceful, and mild-mannered individual. This is a consistent personality style only tested if someone either directly or indirectly hurts, insults, or offends anybody that I love. I can then become unreasonable and deeply unpleasant very, very quickly. I won't repeat what I said to the entitled cow, but needless to say she was shocked that anyone had the balls to challenge her totally unacceptable behaviour with as much vigour as I did that day. I doubt she'll do it again. I am aware that this blip goes against the grain of much of what I have learned, and indeed teach, as an NLP practitioner, but these blips are few and far between, and on that occasion entirely justified.

The performance in between was delightful. Despite the difficult journey, the look of abject joy on my parents' faces throughout made it all worthwhile They loved their granddaughters so much, and they would have moved heaven and earth that day to have seen Isabel perform. They were so very proud, and I was proud of their resilience and determination. They didn't want to travel by car to London, as Dad would have found that more stressful, even with me driving rather than him. They enjoyed people-watching on the trains and, like me, Mum would wonder what other people were up to that day, where they were going, and what sort of lives they had. This is another of those episodes that I look back on with fondness. Most of us as a family were there together that day. And it was only three to four months before they died, so it feels poignant and special.

Christmas soon followed, and we managed to all meet up between Christmas Day and the New Year to enjoy a meal at a restaurant local to Mum and Dad. Reflecting on the photos from that day, Mum was still very much in her element, even though the gradual deterioration of her mobility had resulted in her looking fatigued and somewhat -weary.

Ian and I went away for a long overdue break starting on New Year's Eve, when we visited Lavenham to enjoy dinner with an overnight stay. This was promptly followed by a week-long holiday in St Lucia. That holiday feels like a lifetime ago now. I often reflect on how oblivious we were back then to the collapse of that first domino that had its recent genesis thousands of miles away in Wuhan. An event that was the catalyst that initiated the most horrific chain reaction of harrowing events. We had heard on the news something about a flu-like virus in China that was gathering steady momentum, but it didn't seem real or even relevant to us. I think it was only when infection rates started to rise in places like Italy that we began to realise that Covid-19, the Coronavirus, was going to hit our shores in the United Kingdom. Even then, we definitely didn't have any comprehension that (as of April 2021) nearly 127,000 people in the UK would perish as a result of the virus. Worse still, we never entertained the idea that the virus would wipe out half of the family that I grew up with.

Following our holiday, and upon our return home, Mum had to deal with her most recent medical issue. The circulation in her legs had become progressively worse, and she was now in severe pain. Mum had an extremely high pain threshold, but this was just too much, even for her.

Unfortunately, she had to suffer a series of false dawns with regards to her treatment, and ended up woefully disappointed when the surgical procedures designed to remedy her problem were cancelled at the last minute. I remember driving to the hospital to meet her and Dad before a stent was going to be administered into an artery in her leg. A recent scan had indicated that Mum's arteries in her legs were calcified to 80% and 90% respectively. Now, I am no medical professional, but even I know that this wasn't good, and that if something wasn't done soon Mum was probably going to lose a limb, maybe two.

I was there simply to provide a degree of moral support to my parents, so I was with them when the nurse explained that whilst the surgeon was available to carry out the procedure, there was no bed available for her to recover in afterwards. Mum cried with exasperation, as she had built herself up to this point and managed her pain mentally to cope with it, thinking that there was light at the end of the tunnel.

Sadly, this disappointment soon returned, when Mum finally went in for this procedure and the surgeon announced that he could not proceed because the calcification was too severe and the stent had no chance of 'making it through'. Mum was sent home again, ever more despondent and in a state of despair.

As each delay occurred and the metaphorical can got kicked further down the road, the calendar nudged further into February – just at the time when Covid was creeping further and further towards British soil.

In the meantime, Dad celebrated his 80th birthday on Sunday, 16th February. Conal and I had wanted to plan an 80th birthday party for him, but Dad said he didn't want any fuss. This was a standard and predictable response, but we knew that he would have been privately disappointed had we not made a bit of a fuss of him. So, we set a date for the party, and as Mum's health challenges started to escalate, we took the decision as a family to postpone the celebration until she was better. Instead, we opted for a Thai takeaway at Mum and Dad's house, where we all enjoyed the day, the meal, a few bottles of red, and of course some champagne. It was a lovely day that I look back on so fondly. And I'm pleased that we took photos, as that was the last day that we celebrated as a family.

Ian and I popped back to see them perhaps a week or two later. We had spent the Saturday night with friends on the south coast, and decided to pay Mum and Dad a visit on the way back home. I only mention this because it was the last time that Ian saw Mum alive. When we left, her farewell to Ian struck me as sounding final. I didn't say anything to Ian, or indeed Mum or Dad, at the time, and I wondered whether I had read too much into it. I can't even remember exactly what she said, but it startled me. It was almost as if Mum was expecting something to go wrong and was preparing for the worst. There has always been huge love in our family, to the extent where it was understood and implied rather than expressed verbally. To add context to this, we never really told each other that we loved one another, although there was never any doubt that this was the case. On that day, though, Mum wanted to express that love with a little more resolve than usual. That has stuck with me ever since, and ever so slightly haunts me to this day. And of course, there is a part of me that wonders if I should have been more forthcoming with how I felt about both of them in conversation. Ian then swiftly reminds me that this wasn't necessary, and that it was so astonishingly obvious to anyone how much we loved each other. Its natural to question these things, as it is part of the process of trying to make sense of a situation where sense and logic are in significantly short supply.

Mum finally went in for her surgical procedure shortly afterwards, and this time it finally went ahead. There was a degree of anxiety in the run up to her going in, as she needed a cardiologist to confirm that she was strong enough to sustain the surgery and the anaesthetic. This report came back fine, thankfully, and then the surgery went ahead as planned. I went to visit Mum the day after she had her surgery. The procedure sounded impressive; from what I could understand, they managed to open up the arteries in her legs and clear out the majority of the calcification that had blocked her circulation from functioning properly. When I saw her, I was amazed at how her poor legs had shrunk back to normal size following the procedure. They had been so badly swollen that she'd been in agony, and now blood was given the freedom to flow freely and revitalise a part of her body that had been starved of life for so long. Dad and I were overjoyed to see her in such an improved position. She was still in pain, but it was post-operative pain – healthy recovery pain, if you like – so we weren't too concerned. Instead, we made her as comfortable as possible. I remember calming Mum, and helping her manage her pain by guiding her in meditation. It was so encouraging to see her relax and focus on her breathing as I uttered gentle hypnotic suggestions. Even Dad seemed to relax back into his seat as I continued. I have been meditating for years, and studied the neuroscience of how the brain responds in such circumstances. I was very glad to have such a worthy opportunity to share what I had learned in the hospital with them. I was happy that day, comfortable that everything was heading in the right direction. Dad and I were already discussing the logistics of how we would cope when Mum came back home, whether she would spend some time in a nearby community hospital to rehabilitate first and then come home, supported by a six-week stint of twice daily care support. Dad, whilst being incredibly fit and healthy for an 80-year-old man, did suffer with a bad back. So, we were concerned that if he hurt his back whilst helping Mum to the toilet, we would be in all sorts of trouble. In fact, only a week before, my friend David and I had run the Brentwood Half Marathon and popped in to check on Dad to see how he was whilst Mum was in hospital. We caught him trying to manoeuvre a mattress from their bedroom to the lounge downstairs. We got there in time to help him, and warned him not to try anything like that again.

Over the next couple of days, Mum's surgical wounds were healing up quite nicely, but she started to come down with post-operative pneumonia. She was tested for Covid and, thankfully, the result was negative. I remember how relieved I was to hear this news, as we understandably feared for the worst. I recall how jubilant I felt that day, because it coincided with receiving the encouraging news from his oncologist that his cancer had not returned. I posted a celebratory update on Facebook, announcing what for us as a family was a significant double victory. The rationale behind my post was not only to brief my family and friends on Mum and Dad's health progressions, but also to spread some hope and positivity at a time when fear was beginning to tighten its grip on the morale of my wider online community. I am going to be completely and utterly honest with you now and admit that as I posted that announcement, I wondered fleetingly whether I was tempting fate. I've never verbalised that dormant thought before, but it feels natural to do so now. Given the events that followed, it's quite natural to succumb to the ifs, buts, and maybes that encourage superstitious musings. I don't let it bother me at all, but the thought was very much alive in my head.

Unfortunately, our celebrations were short-lived. Mum was becoming more and more distressed day after day. Conal, Dad, and I had set up a WhatsApp group, which became our forum for sharing quick messages and updates in between more detailed updates shared via telephone. I could sense that

Dad was becoming concerned as Mum's cognitive abilities took a nosedive, leading her into a state of delirium. Having tested negative for Covid, we just thought that Mum's pneumonia, or perhaps an infection elsewhere, was causing her confusion. The situation rapidly deteriorated, though, and it was at this point that a second Covid test was ordered. This time our worst fears were realised when the test came back positive. By this time, the UK Government had introduced a national lockdown, and one of the consequences of this was that all hospitals had to close their doors to all visitors. This meant that even Dad had to stay at home and receive updates from the hospital as and when they became available. This was incredibly difficult for Dad, who had been by her side every previous day in hospital, for up to 12 hours at a time. I know that he was heartbroken to be at home and not be with Mum, particularly as this coincided with her testing positive for Covid. Conal had already warned me in the weeks leading up to this point that if Mum contracted the virus, it would be extremely unlikely that she would survive.

On the evening of Friday, 27th March, Ian and I decided to distract ourselves by attending a 'Zoom drink' with some friends from our local business community. Zoom drinks had become the new way of connecting socially during lockdown, and it took off relatively quickly. We enjoyed a well needed catch-up with our friends that evening, and then went to bed exhausted by the week's events.

I generally sleep very well and am a morning lark! I like to go to bed early (by about 10pm) and get up at around 5:30am. Add about an hour to that schedule for the weekend, and it's about right. I don't need an alarm, as I wake up naturally at the time that I need to each day. On Saturday, 28th March, 2020, I woke up naturally at 6am, and within minutes I glanced at my phone and saw Conal's name appear on a phone that had its volume turned to silent. I knew instantly that something was wrong. I think that most of us now are alert to phone calls that are received out of context, either from people who don't normally call us (maybe they email, text or WhatsApp instead) or perhaps from close family members but at unusual times of the day. 6:12am on a Saturday morning is high alert time for me, regardless of who is calling. I knew instinctively that my life was about to change forever.

I answered the call and could tell that Conal was driving and speaking to me via Bluetooth. He told me that the doctor looking after Mum had called Conal to warn him that her breathing had become very shallow, and she was deteriorating quickly. Given Conal's status as an NHS consultant, he was the natural liaison for the medical staff to contact whenever there were any developments. Conal would then triage and filter the communication to me and Dad, so that we understood what was happening, how serious it was, and whether we needed to do anything to help support the situation. It was clear from Conal's tone of voice that this was a serious deterioration, and that I needed to jump in my car and get to the hospital as quickly as possible. The journey from my house to the hospital is about an hour, so I set off promptly, and I don't remember how I got there. I must have zoned out and entered a trance as I navigated myself to the hospital. I parked the car and then called Conal, who had arrived half an hour earlier than me. But we were both too late; Conal told me that Mum was gone. Adrenaline immediately kicked in, and I acknowledged what I had been told, and arranged to meet my brother at the ward where Mum had died.

Within a matter of minutes, I had to vocalise 'My mum has just died' three times. First, to Ian, who I rang as I approached the hospital reception area. I can still hear how surprised he was as I told him; the adrenaline rush must have put me into a focused mindset, and I might have sounded a little matter of fact in the way that I told him. Perhaps not; I don't really know. But he was shocked. I think he thought that I would at least get there and have a chance to say goodbye to Mum, so to hear that I had found out and not even set foot in the hospital was a big shock. The second person I had to tell was the security guard who was stopping the public from entering the building. I uttered those words again, and he let me in and directed me to the ward. I was now on autopilot, just as I had been in the car on the way there. The third person was the ward nurse who must have seen me wander in looking confused and in a daze, and she gently ushered me in the right direction. I will never forget the slow-motion event of me walking along a ward corridor that was on a bend, and seeing my brother emerge as I approached. As our eyes locked, the stark reality of the horror of the situation pulverised me, and I momentarily burst into tears before composing myself to greet Conal.

Almost silently, a nurse assisted me with my PPE and ushered Conal and me into the ward where Mum lay behind a screen accompanied by a wooden flower that would have been repeatedly used by the hospital to symbolise and recognise a death. Nothing prepares you for this – nothing! Even now, a year later, as I type this sentence tears of sorrow and disbelief run down my cheeks when I cast my mind back to this moment. Conal and I caught each other's gaze as we stood either side of Mum. We didn't need to say anything to one another to understand what the other was thinking and feeling. Conal and I have an almost telepathic understanding of one another under normal circumstances. Now, in the most intense life-changing scenario that either of us had ever experienced, we both knew in intimate detail instinctively what the other was thinking. We stood there for a while; I have no idea for how long. Time suspends itself in a vacuum when something like this happens.

I collected her bag of belongings from her bedside, and then bade her farewell by placing my gloved hand on her cheek.

I couldn't even kiss her forehead, such was the risk of viral transmission. Not only had this fucking virus killed my mother, but it had done so without even giving us the chance to say goodbye, to comfort our mother before she passed, nor even kiss her forehead. The cruelty of this situation is off the scale, and it wasn't about to get any better.

How the fuck do we tell Dad that his wife has just died? This was our next challenge. We agreed that Conal would call Dad to tell him what had happened, whilst I drove to see him. The journey from the hospital to Dad's house was just shy of 15 minutes, and Conal kept him on the phone until I arrived. It is so cruel that our poor father had to hear the news that his beloved wife had died from his son over the phone, and then all his other son could do upon arrival was comfort him with words from the other side of a window. I couldn't enter the house, as the risk of transmission was too great either way. Dad wasn't displaying symptoms at this point, so we had no idea that he had already caught the virus from Mum. As such, there was a risk, but we didn't know from whom. I will forever be haunted by the look of abject shock and disbelief on Dad's face as I spoke to him through the window. He was utterly broken and almost childlike in his weakened state. All I wanted to do was to hug and hold him tight, to tell him that I understood how awful and devastating this situation was, but that I would always be there for him and would never leave his side.

When I drove back home later that day, I spent the journey calling my closest friends to brief them on my news. Again, I can recall each conversation, and am grateful to my friends for their support. I knew instinctively that the road ahead was going to be difficult as, given the lockdown, I would not have support in the physical sense from family or friends, and that contact would be virtually and over the phone. I needed to start putting together my support bubble for the hard days ahead, and I didn't delay in doing this. By that point, adrenaline had kicked in, and my energy levels spiked as I spent the whole day on the phone communicating our news to relatives and friends far and wide. It's such an intense process, and feels like you are working full pelt as a kind of executive personal assistant. The phone kept pinging with texts, WhatsApp and Facebook messages, and phone calls, and I took pride in keeping on top of them all. At a moment when my world had spiralled out of control, this was one way that I could reintroduce an element of control. Of course, it was so lovely to hear from family and friends, and I certainly enjoyed those conversations. Dad was in too much shock to field them, and I triaged the contact from family so that he wasn't overwhelmed. In the afternoon of that day, the calls starting slowly making their way to Dad.

The days that followed were awash with cards, gifts, flowers, wine, messages, and calls to me, Dad, and Conal – all of which were gratefully received. I can say with hand on heart that the messages of support that made their way to me during this period kept my spirits up. I don't believe in coincidence; each message landed with me at just the right moment, almost intuitively.

And then the administration process presented itself to us. This is another way to start taking back a little control. I volunteered to arrange the funeral, so early the following week I was in discussions with the funeral plan provider, the church, funeral director, and florist. All of this, of course, was during a national lockdown, making the process more complex in some respects and unfortunately simpler in others. We could only have ten people at the funeral, as that was the local authority's restriction number.

Naturally, I took time away from work for a few days, and gradually stepped back to just dealing with back-office events and keeping myself away from client contact. I wasn't ready to face people who weren't family and friends, and I needed to keep myself strong for Dad, who was still in shock and constantly in tears. He was heartbroken that his wife of 52 years had passed away without him being by her side. Not saying goodbye is so cruel and unfair. It makes you contemplate conversations that you wish you'd had. None of us got to say goodbye to Mum, and we can only hope that she wasn't in too much distress as the virus took hold of her.

In the days and weeks that followed, I coped – supported by my husband Ian, my brother Conal, and my dad. We supported each other, and our family and friends kept close to us virtually, if not physically. I balanced out my coping mechanisms by drinking and eating heavily, and then going out running most mornings to clear my head, enjoy some fresh air, and get blood pumping around my body. As a reasonably short-term measure, it worked for me. It's not a long-term strategy, but right then it was exactly what I needed to do. It was not the time to start trying to become clever by dipping into my 'toolkit' of coaching strategies. That had its place a little later on, as you will come to see.

It is no surprise to me that this chapter is the longest of the book, because this was the beginning of the events that would change our lives forever. Our mother was a formidable woman who fought illness and health challenges time and time again, but always maintained a resilient spirit and never gave up. I am proud to be her son, and will always think of her with an immense sense of pride, love, and gratitude. Christine Dympna Perrett, 13/12/1942 to 28/03/2020. May you rest in peace forever.

Chapter 6

2020: Dad

Our mother's untimely death took us completely by surprise. We weren't ready for it, even though in the run-up to her death, Conal and I privately felt an impending sense of doom.

Nothing, however, came close to preparing us for the abject horror that was to follow in the three-week period that lay ahead. Even one year later, as I write this chapter, I pause momentarily to wonder at the dramatic turn of events that shook, tore, and devastated the foundations of our family forever.

Losing Dad – an otherwise fit, agile, nimble, and healthy 80-year-old was never on our radar; it was simply inconceivable that there was even the remotest possibility of that. Tragically, however, that is precisely what happened, as my worst nightmare emerged into the most unforgiving of realities.

Dad's devotion to Mum was palpable to anyone and everyone. In over 50 years of marriage, they spent the majority of their non-working time together, always in each other's company. Upon reflection, this was probably not the healthiest strategy, as they bickered quite a lot, but no more than any other couple that spent so much time together.

Mum was totally dependent upon Dad to look after her, particularly in her last decade of life. She didn't like the fact, because even during her lowest physical ebb, following or indeed preceding one of her many surgical procedures, her independent spirit was acute and alert.

Consequently, Dad sadly had much of his freedom in later life curtailed by his increasingly demanding role as Mum's carer. This wasn't a role that he had prepared for or been trained for, but it was one that he embraced naturally and organically, driven by his unswerving loyalty and love for his wife.

It is deeply and tragically ironic that this devotion ultimately led to our father's death. Every day since Mum had been admitted to hospital, Dad spent probably eight hours with her, by her bedside, helping her to eat and drink, keeping her entertained with conversation, updates about what Conal and I were up to, and of course what was going on in the world – including how the Coronavirus was beginning to take its grip on the nation.

Dad contracted Covid-19 from our mother in the short window between Mum testing positive and the hospital closing its doors to the public and visitors of dying relatives. Dad was truly devastated by Mum's death, utterly devastated, and was a broken man in the days that followed. He did manage to muster sufficient energy to discuss Mum's funeral arrangements with Conal and me. And we spoke to him at length about the future, hoping to help him visualise that life could eventually go on. Dad was committed to Conal and me; he loved us dearly and would have wanted to carry on, clawing back some of his life in his twilight years. He lived also for his grandchildren, Isabel and Georgia. We talked about him spending time with Conal, Miranda, and the girls in their house in London, taking the girls to and from school, and on trips to museums. He would have loved that, and it would have kept his spirits sustainably high for many years.

However, within a few days, Dad appeared to develop what seemed like a cold. We didn't think that it was anything more than that. He had been alone in his house since Mum had been admitted to hospital. We didn't at first appreciate that he could have contracted the virus during the very short window between Mum testing positive and him not being allowed to visit her. As the days progressed, however, his temperature began to steadily rise, and his night sweats began to take a grip on him. He had to change his bed sheets each day, as they were saturated with sweat. Conal and I would share the responsibility of visiting him and bringing him food, whilst the neighbours also did the same to help us. Thankfully, Dad's appetite seemed okay, but we were becoming increasingly concerned that he had, in fact, caught the virus.

At first, when it looked like he had contracted Covid, we thought that it might be a good thing so that he could promptly recover without fuss, and develop the antibodies which would protect him from future infection. Sadly, the virus was far more aggressive than we had anticipated, and it just would not let him go. Each day was tortuous, trying to anticipate and predict what was going to happen next. Dad was fastidious in his note-taking, and twice daily took his temperature, marking the results on his pad and updating Conal and me via WhatsApp. I still have the pad here by my side, and can see Dad's handwriting and the date next to each entry. The increase in temperature was so gradual, with the occasional drop, that it was impossible to predict an outcome. He must have been exhausted, as his sleep was beginning to suffer. He had never been the best sleeper, often waking up in the middle of the night and being unable to go back to sleep, but now he was getting hardly any sleep, which was a huge concern to us. His immune system needed as much natural support as possible, and sleep would at least offer his body a chance to strengthen itself overnight. Without it, he was running seriously short of artillery.

On Easter Saturday, Conal and his daughters visited Dad, to take him soup and other healthy and nutritious food. Later that day, Conal rang me, and it was obvious that he was driving. He told me that he had taken Dad back with him to London, as he was struggling with his breathing, and Conal felt he could make him more comfortable by taking him up to the hospital where he worked in London, and where his colleagues could support him with some oxygen. Conal sounded very relaxed and positive, but I knew that he had to do that because Dad was sitting next to him, and Isabel and Georgia were also in the car. There was no way he was going to say anything that would alarm any of them, but I could clearly read between the lines and knew that Dad had taken a turn for the worse.

Dad was made comfortable and placed on a CPAP machine to assist his breathing. At no point did he go onto a ventilator; his medical team preferring to assist him more gently with the CPAP, constantly monitoring his oxygen saturation levels, and trying to stabilise him so that he could mount a recovery. As this was my brother's professional territory, it was easier to obtain updates, and Conal relayed the information back to me on a daily basis. Visitors weren't allowed, apart from Conal, so Ian and I would regularly FaceTime Dad to lift his spirits; we even drove to his house on a beautifully sunny day and FaceTimed him from the garden, after we had cut the grass and watered the lawn. The weather during that lockdown was amazing, with sunshine on an almost daily basis and temperatures that soared into the seventies.

The days that followed were difficult. It was becoming increasingly difficult to predict the outcome of Dad's ordeal.

Each day, we keenly awaited Dad's oxygen saturation results, his temperature, and his overall wellbeing, including the condition of his vital organs. Each day, the results fluctuated, making it extremely difficult to formulate any form of assessment. To complicate matters further, on the days that Dad's statistics looked the bleakest, he appeared to be better to us as we FaceTimed him. I recall one day in particular when he finally managed to get out of bed and was sitting up in his chair speaking to me and waving. I was utterly convinced on that day that he was getting better. *The stats must be wrong or misleading*, I thought; *they must be a blip, and tomorrow Dad is going to get better.* It was so awful, because I was communicating to family and friends and updating them each day, and I started to feel guilty that the information that I was supplying was misleading them. At one point, I told a relative that as long as he continued to improve beyond the weekend, he would probably come home the following week. Dad's chance of survival was now well and truly on a knife edge. I was, of course, only feeding back the information that I was being given myself, and relaying my observations, but I felt bad that I had got it so badly wrong.

I am by nature an optimist, and I wondered if my optimism was feeding my confirmation bias to create unrealistic outcome chains in my brain. Looking back now, it was the most natural thing in the world to feel that way. I had just lost my mother and it was unfathomable to consider that I might be days away from losing Dad. It now became more difficult to contact him, as he was starting to fail, and answering his phone was a task that was fast becoming beyond him. I still sent him messages, desperately hoping that he might read them and feel inspired enough to respond, or more importantly rally and fight the crippling virus that had diseased his body, forcing it into frailty. I had heard that he was struggling to get a decent night's sleep, and I remember frantically posting on Facebook for support amongst my personal development community; I was trying to find a way to filter gentle meditative and hypnotic sounds, music, and narrative, to help usher him into a good night's sleep. Despite the tidal wave of supportive suggestions that arrived, I privately felt that this was all too little too late. At that point, I felt completely impotent, and resigned myself to reacting to news as it came in from my brother, potentially preparing myself mentally for the worst-case scenario.

On Tuesday, 21st April, Conal called me to let me know that the respiratory team looking after Dad were concerned that his stats weren't improving, and that it was unlikely that they were going to improve. They were becoming anxious that his organs might be starting to fail as his body continued to put up a fight. That day, Conal and I were given the option of making a brutally difficult decision. To keep Dad on respiratory support, with him slipping in and out of consciousness and his body failing each day; an outcome that would almost certainly end in his eventual death – perhaps conscious of his demise, and potentially in extreme distress. Or to remove the CPAP machine that was gently assisting his breathing, and let him peacefully slip away. This is not a discussion that anybody should ever have to make on behalf of a loved one, and to this day it sends a terse shiver down my spine simply thinking about it.

Conal and I made a unanimous decision to agree with the Respiratory Consultant that was supervising Dad's care, and take him off what was in fact his life support machine. We decided to commence that process on the following day, and Conal suggested to me that I might want to come up to the hospital in London and see Dad one last time. We were both conscious of the fact that we didn't get to Mum in time before her death, so this time we weren't going to take any chances. I concluded that it would be better for me to go to the hospital under controlled circumstances, and say goodbye to my father before the respiratory support had been withdrawn. We agreed that Conal would come back the following day and marshal that event.

The drive from my house to the hospital in London is probably 90 minutes. I figured that I would call some of my closest friends on the way up there, which I did. 'I'm on my way up to the hospital in London to say goodbye to Dad,' I was still running on adrenaline at this point, and I guess you kind of go into automatic pilot mode. I wasn't in hysterics, but calmly focused, whilst letting my subconscious get me to where I needed to be. It comforted me to speak to friends on the way up there. From memory, I spoke to Catherine, Marcos, David Liddle, and David Fitzgerald. These conversations were interspersed with brief update calls to and from Conal, so that I could provide my 'ETA'.

I parked up in a side street and agreed to meet my brother in the reception lobby of the hospital. I wasn't supposed to be there, as we were still in a fierce lockdown with no visitors permitted into the hospital. A combination of Dad's bleak outlook and kind intervention from the staff on Dad's ward, though, meant that I could join Conal by his bedside. Before I could see Dad, I was taken into a side room by some nursing staff who helped me get into my protective clothing. I guess this process took about ten minutes, but it felt like an hour. I could tell from the look in the nurses' eyes that they knew that I was heading in to say goodbye. They were respectfully kind and gentle with me, whilst determined to protect me from the viral load that was in brutal occupation of the Covid ward. Every connecting piece of fabric was tightly taped together with its counterpart. Even my protective gloves were taped over the sleeves of my gown to ensure that nothing could breach the barrier. A protective visor then was positioned over my head and face, which already had a face mask.

I was led into the room, and I was immediately struck by the grave danger facing everyone on this ward. Nobody was in there that didn't need to be. I felt like I was stuck centre stage in the middle of a horror film; a catastrophe movie; dying, vulnerable people meeting my every glance. I was then greeted with the sight of my poor father in his bed, his breathing now supported fully by the CPAP. I have mentioned already that it was a hot summer, and that particular week was punctuated by high temperatures and sunshine. I was melting in my PPE, and my previous calm state had abandoned me. I started hyperventilating, which caused my visor to steam up. I know that Conal could see I was distressed, but I was determined to maintain my composure for Dad's sake, Conal's sake, and for my own. I was about to define history and create a memory that was destined to remain with me for the rest of my life. Now was not the time to fuck this up.

Over the years I have learned an abundance of strategies and techniques to assist with grounding, maintaining composure, dealing with anxiety, fight, flight or freeze dilemmas, and now I was being severely tested. I knew what was at stake, and my subconscious didn't let me down. I can remember concentrating on my breathing and turning an imaginary 'volume dial' down from 10 to 1 in my head. My racing pulse started to stabilise. I caught Conal's eye and, despite him remaining silent, I could sense his compassion, which also helped to keep me grounded. I sat down in a chair next to Dad and held his hand with my gloved hand. I was struck immediately by how warm his hand was, and it reminded me that he was still alive. I looked up and saw his face, eyes shut, and breathing supported by a machine. I squeezed his hand and looked for a physical response, but there was none.

The nurse who had accompanied Conal and me to Dad's bedside sensed that I was about to say goodbye and gently reassured me that he could in all probability hear what I was about to say. I hadn't rehearsed anything at all, and even if I had I would have ended up saying something completely different. I took a deep breath, and then words just seemed to naturally utter from my mouth; a spontaneous flow of words thanking my father for being there for me from the day that I was born, up to the current day; for always loving and supporting me, and always, always standing by my side through thick and thin. I warmly told him how proud I was of him, and that he inspired me with his kindness, wisdom, and commitment. I congratulated him on the impact that he'd had on Conal and me, that we would always remember him with the deepest love and compassion, and that he could hold his head high and take comfort in the reality that we loved him so, so much, and that despite what was about to happen he would never die in my heart.

I looked at Conal, who nodded reassuringly at me, suggesting that I had said everything that Dad needed to hear. He also reaffirmed the nurse's feeling that Dad would have heard every word I had said. I hope that he did, and that my words comforted him as he neared his death. Even though I can't know for sure, and it broke my heart that – like with Mum – I didn't have a chance to say a proper farewell involving a two-way conversation, I choose to think that he heard every word. Maybe one day I'll know for sure...

I drove home in a trance; I finally got there at around 10pm, and stopped only once to buy a bottle of vodka. I wouldn't normally drink on a school night, but I didn't care, and all of my routines and schedules had gone out of the window, at least for the time being. Upon arrival, I could hear Ian crying as he was chatting to his friend Chrissie on the phone. I then turned to see one of my favourite photos of Dad printed out and placed on our dining room table, surrounded by candles. A vigil, sadly not of hope but of peaceful acceptance of what was about to follow. I then spent the remainder of the evening drinking with Ian, listening to music, and chatting until 4am.

The following day, I vaguely remember doing a bit of behind the scenes work to keep my mind occupied, but not anything stressful (this is how I worked for the few months that surrounded this period), and then Conal headed into the hospital in the afternoon to say his farewell and to sit with Dad as the support was withdrawn. I notified my second cousin, Canon Martin Downey, who is based in Galway, and he said Last Rites.

At 6:35pm on Wednesday, 22nd April, Conal called me to say that our dad, Brian Clifford Perrett, had passed away. I was numb for a while, and then the adrenaline kicked in once again. I had relied heavily on social media throughout this crisis to keep family and friends far and wide updated of what was happening, so I posted a tribute to Dad online and then the messages and calls started filtering in. I opened a bottle of wine, and then hit the phone and started updating my family. This time, I think I was in bed by midnight.

My father had died, and now only Conal and I remained from the family that we were brought up in. The dynamic of our immediate family set-up had changed forever. I had still been processing our mother's death at that point, and now this.

Rest in Peace, Dad, we love you and miss you more than you can possibly imagine.

Brian Clifford Perrett – 16/02/1940 to 22/04/2020.

Chapter 7

The Funeral

We had originally set a date for Mum's funeral of April 15th. As Dad's condition worsened, we had to consider postponing Mum's funeral, as it was unthinkable that Dad would miss it. We knew he would never forgive himself, and we didn't want him to experience any stress whilst he was ill. I remember calling the undertaker and nervously asking how long we could postpone the funeral for. I recall panicking, because I had forgotten to inform the florist of the delay until a week beforehand. Thankfully, my mind was quickly put at rest, as Jan from the Funeral Directors advised me that I didn't need to worry; we could simply wait until Dad was better and then set a fresh date for the funeral. She also capably dealt with the florist, who then graciously awaited further instructions. It still felt really odd to be having these conversations, and I actually felt like I was being a nuisance by having to change the date. Of course, nobody made me feel that way at all. It was maybe my way of trying to feel normal amid a markedly abnormal set of circumstances.

We had already been advised that for Mum's funeral we had a numbers limit of ten people. This was an extraordinary position to be in, as in essence this meant that we had to stick to mine and Conal's immediate family, perhaps with a couple of places to spare. I didn't even know if we could have any more friends or family in the cemetery, but distanced from the grave. As it transpired, this was indeed possible in Brentwood. It was fairly confusing, because each town had its own set of rules, governed of course by the relevant council. When it became apparent that Dad wasn't going to recover, we had the most unusual task of having to consider the prospect of a 'double funeral'. Again, I called Jan to advise her of Dad's death. and I actually felt slightly nervous before calling her. because I was about to deliver bad news again and I was conscious of how this might make her feel. I know, it's bizarre. but that is how I managed to keep on top of the situation – by not shutting out normality, and maintaining reactions to circumstances that felt natural to me.

The funeral of both our parents was set for 9:30am on Thursday, 7th May, 2020. I was dreading the funeral, and struggled mentally in the days leading up to it. It felt like the culmination of the worst time of our lives, and I assumed that it would be an excruciatingly difficult day, with little in the way of redeeming features. The restrictions on numbers in the cemetery, social distancing, and saying goodbye to both of my beloved parents all at once, seemed unbearable and impossible to comprehend. And of course, it still does – very little of what has happened makes any sense. Fortunately, all of the arrangements were meticulously in place, and Ian and I had driven to Mum and Dad's house the evening before and prepared the garden for the few guests that we would be welcoming back to the house afterwards for refreshments.

Surrounding the chaos, pain, heartache, devastation, sadness, and loss was the most empowering sphere of love, connection, memories, nostalgia, kindness, and generosity of spirit. The latter is stronger than the former, which is why I can confidently assert that the day ended with far more positive emotions than it did negative. And I can be extremely grateful for this...

The closest members of my family assembled at my parents' house in Brentwood on the morning of the funeral, and at 9am the hearses arrived. They paused at the house for a few moments, as all of the neighbours congregated. The street holds over 80 houses, and every neighbour from every house lined the whole road with a guard of honour. As the funeral cortege then slowly headed towards the cemetery, the whole street erupted with respectful applause. My parents had lived in the same house since 1972, when Conal was a baby and before I was born, and must have been one of the earliest residents of the street. We were only expecting perhaps a handful of immediate neighbours to pay their respects – certainly not the entire street. And we will never forget this overwhelming display of love and support! We were completely and utterly blown away by it. The message was clear to us: Mum and Dad were loved by so many in the neighbourhood. We had seen this when Mum died, and now it could not have been more evident.

I needn't have dreaded the funeral at all. The cemetery at Woodman Road is situated in a beautiful, intimate, wooded space, and it helped that the weather was perfect, with a clear blue sky and unbridled sunshine. The plot itself is situated a few spaces away from the father of one of my oldest friends, which I found most reassuring. The service was beautiful, and ended with a song and a poem from my two darling nieces, Isabel and Georgia. They were only aged nine and seven at the time, so they were incredibly courageous to offer such a charming contribution under such difficult circumstances. The graveside service was conducted by Father Gary Dench from Brentwood Cathedral. I had established a good relationship with Father Gary in the preceding weeks, and he delivered a service that provided our family with great comfort. I was also very grateful to the Funeral Directors Cribb & Sons, who fully supported us through all of the funeral arrangements, taking away a huge amount of stress and anxiety.

After the service finished and our parents were laid to rest, a small number of us returned to my parents' house, where we enjoyed some food and raised a toast to our Mum and Dad. I wouldn't normally drink champagne at 10:30am, but I was certainly ready for it that day. For the next few hours, we shared stories about Mum and Dad, and laughed hysterically as we recalled many hilarious moments over the years.

At 2pm, we then watched the online memorial service kindly delivered by my cousin Canon Martin Downey, live from St Joseph's Church in Galway. This was an apt and appreciated conclusion to the formal part of the day's events, listening to Father Martin share fondly remembered stories from when my mother was a young girl and then meeting my father for the first time. Conal and I were so grateful to Martin for his love and support.

After the service, we all parted ways, and Ian and I headed home. Our friends Mark and Neil followed us back to Braintree, and joined us for a drink in our back garden. The day concluded with Ian and I joining a Zoom get-together with a group of our friends. This had been organised as a separate event from the funeral, and chatting with them offered me a welcome distraction and rounded off the day nicely. Despite the circumstances, the funeral went well and was a good day. I look back on it with only fond memories.

Chapter 8

Aftermath and Future

The weeks that followed the funeral ushered in a quiet period where life began to creep every so slowly into 'some semblance of normality'. Well, not really, but that's how I thought I was expected to feel. I will explore this further in Part 2 of this book, but essentially the funeral feels like the final stage of the current phase of mourning. We continued dealing with the mountain of paperwork involving our parents' estate at that point. Bank accounts, insurance policies, pensions, investments, utility companies, council tax, and of course kicking off the probate process. I found dealing with all of this quite therapeutic, and it gave me a sense of purpose.

I was back at work pretty much full time by now, albeit still working from home. This was handy as I was mentally and physically exhausted, so being able to walk a few feet from my office to my bedroom to take a 30-minute nap at 3pm was useful, and something which would have raised an eyebrow had I done the same in our office in Chelmsford. Much of my time at work at that time involved minimal client exposure, and I cherry-picked who I spoke to. Many of our clients are also friends, so it was these people that I spoke to, as I would naturally have valued their time and could be myself. I avoided speaking to new clients for a few weeks, because I found it disingenuous to pretend that everything was fine when it wasn't. Make no mistake, just because the funeral day went well, does not mean that I was okay and getting back to normal – far from it! I have dealt with my grief admirably, but it's been a bloody long hard slog that has taken me over a year to smooth some of the most heavily serrated edges, and of course it's an ongoing process.

One aspect that I found particularly challenging was adjusting to life as the voices around me began to quieten. When something this dramatic happens, your community rises up to support you – the majority of this was online, given the lockdown restrictions. After the funeral, it became quiet apart from a few check-in messages, predominantly from those who'd had similar experiences to me in their past. This is completely natural, but it did act as a catalyst to feelings of paranoia and mind reading that I will explore later in the book. As I write this chapter, we are emerging from the most pernicious second wave, and are exiting lockdown. The vaccination program is in full flow, and it looks and feels like we are heading on the right trajectory. There is still a universal sensation of anxiety that we might experience another false dawn, and this is perhaps preventing us all from relaxing completely. It's incredible what you learn to live with, so I can only begin to imagine how joyous an occasion it will be when we all start to meet up again and go on international holidays. Hopefully, we won't take any of this for granted again.

In the months that followed the funeral, Ian and I spent an increasing amount of time with my brother Conal, his wife Miranda, and my nieces, Isabel and Georgia. We would meet every Sunday at our parents' house and enjoy a barbecue together. This played a huge role for us all in our healing process. To meet up and enjoy great food, wine, and each other's company in the garden of Mum and Dad's house, in the beautiful sunshine, was a saving grace that I am so grateful for. 2020 was an abomination in so many ways, but the consolation prize of one of the hottest summers since records began in the UK took the edge off a little. Since then, we have all met up whenever there has been a reason to reflect or celebrate. And of course, then begins the bittersweet pattern of experiencing the 'firsts' of all of the major milestones. Soon after the funeral we had Father's Day, then my 46th birthday, Mum and Dad's wedding anniversary, Conal's birthday, Mum's birthday, Christmas, New Year, Dad's birthday, Mother's Day, and then the first anniversaries of Mum and Dad's deaths. Spending as many of those days together helped to stop in its tracks a tsunami of grief that had been gathering perpetual momentum and was causing a considerable amount of anxiety in the run up to each and every one of these events.

By the time July approached, I had my business mojo back and I was raring to go. My business partner David Liddle and I run four businesses, and the pandemic had forced us – like many others – to make swift and courageous decisions to protect the financial integrity of our businesses and keep our clients and staff safe. We dealt with all of this admirably and took it all in our stride. My attitude towards business challenges had shifted, and the majority of my fear and limiting beliefs evaporated as my renewed confidence helped me to stride into situations – good, bad, or indifferent – with a mentality to resolve, improve, and excel. Throughout that summer leading up to the autumn, our sales figures surged as we clawed back the momentum that we had lost at the start of the lockdown. My attitude was that I had already experienced the most harrowing and horrific set of circumstances that I am every likely to have, so in reality there was nothing to fear. I cannot be hurt in the same way that I have already been hurt, so why not recognise my goals? Why not visualise my goals? Why not dream and aspire without limitation?

I took this time also to expand my repertoire in personal development. Over a three-month window following Mum and Dad's funeral, I completed my coaching credentials and became an accredited and licensed coach with the International Coaching Federation. I participated in a Core Transformation course, learning how to embrace Peace, Oneness, and Love, by using a beautiful NLP technique that I continue using to this day and will do so forever in the future. And then my proudest moment, which was to become a Master Practitioner in Hypnotherapy. I dedicated this achievement to my parents, as it means so much to me. I had planned to become a hypnotherapist many months beforehand, as I wanted to help Mum manage her relationship with pain, and although she died before I qualified, I know that she would have been so very proud of me. She would have encouraged me to use my new skill to help others manage their challenges, whether that be pain, emotions, limiting beliefs, smoking cessation, weight loss, or indeed grief. This period of personal and professional development helped me navigate a very difficult period of my life, and I have grown as a person as a direct and indirect consequence of it. I trusted my subconscious to direct my decision-making process, and I was rewarded with a summer of fulfilment.

In July, Ian and I welcomed Toby into our family. Toby is our Beagle/Pointer puppy. I had never owned a dog before, although Ian had, and despite the hair-raising initial few months, Toby became part of our family and is loved so much. He has helped me with my grief, because he gave me a focus for my love, someone to look after and protect, and someone who would show me unconditional love in return. I'll remind myself of this of course next time he wakes me up at 3am, ostensibly to go to the loo, but in reality just because he's awake and wants my attention. Moving forward into 2021, I then expanded our businesses further, taking on more staff in our new, larger office. I started writing this book, which then inspired me to finish it and establish a process for promoting and marketing it, so that it could support our Identity Resource business as well as its primary goal of inspiring those who choose to read it. I launched a podcast, where I interview people from all walks of life who have inspired me with their stories of courage, compassion, and determination. I have a second book waiting to be written, and now intend to write one book per year as a standard goal. I have continued to raise the bar of my standards and am enjoying every moment. I have coached individuals and businesses throughout this period, empowering them to make strong decisions about their direction in life that work well for them, first and foremost. And I have many other aspirations involving music and business that I will share over the coming months that I am truly excited about.

I mention all of this not to boast or brag; this is not about ego for me. I derive so much joy from all of these activities that I don't need external validation. For me, this is about as liberating as it gets. I mention all of this to inspire and to motivate, and to send a very clear message to all those reading that no matter what happens in life we all have the resources within us to emerge stronger. Make no mistake – life will not become easy for me moving forward. This is not the last tragic event that is likely to happen to me. I am not immune from sorrow. What I am, however, is positioned in the most resilient chamber of optimism that it is highly unlikely my spirit will ever be broken. If that is the case for me, then there is no reason whatsoever that it should be any different for you.

I began to realise and appreciate how precious life is, and that there is no room for self-limiting beliefs. We have to 'seize the day' and extrapolate the joy and awe from every moment, whilst taking time – even briefly – to wonder and be grateful. Our talents, personalities, characteristics, relationships, and opportunities are gifts not to be squandered or wasted, but to be recognised, cultivated, and nurtured. I often refer to this period of my life as a period of 'Post Traumatic Growth'.

I guess this is a positive reframe of the Post Traumatic Stress Disorder that I experienced (which I refer to in Part 2), and it rests on the principle that 'If I am going to feel this bad, I might as well get something out of it'. This has been an epiphany for me, because if I can find something positive to emerge from such a dark period of my life, this has to be a most significant life lesson. Bizarrely, so much good has emerged as a result of this tragedy, and I have evolved and grown as a person. In essence, I learned not just to bounce back; I learned how to bounce forward.

The future for me now looks exciting, awash with opportunity and purpose. I am motivated by my values of Growth, Contribution, Love, and Connection. I am no longer driven by Significance and Certainty. The future is my responsibility, and mine only. By taking ownership of my destiny, owning my mistakes, being clear on what I want in life, and even clearer about what I don't want, I have the opportunity to lead the most fulfilling and richly rewarding life that I could ever hope for.

The tragedy that I have experienced will not scar or embitter me, nor will it become a barrier or obstacle to the achievement of my dreams and aspirations. It will, however, and does empower me to be the best version of myself. To remove doubt and fear so that I can stride confidently towards a life that I deserve. I can do this empowered by the strongest psychological anchor, and that is the clearest, most vivid memory and vision of my dearly beloved parents smiling at me and wishing me the happiest most fulfilled life, and knowing that by achieving this I will in turn make them the happiest and proudest parents that a son could ever hope to wish for.

Part Two – Introduction

In Part Two, I will share my experiences with you as I embarked upon my own personal odyssey through the Kubler-Ross Grief cycle. Elizabeth Kubler-Ross was a Swiss-American psychiatrist who developed a theory of the five stages of grief. The reason that I am sharing this with you is to help you understand that it is completely natural to experience each and every one of these stages. It is also completely natural to experience only some of them. There is no order in which you experience them, and no set time that you will sit in that zone. You may experience one far more intensely than the others, and you will most likely dart between them.

If, by baring my soul to you and being completely honest with you about how I felt at each stage, I can help you appreciate that you are not alone, then I will have succeeded in my quest in writing this book. Part One was essential in telling the story and providing context, as well as hopefully concluding with a compelling sense of hope and inspiration. Part Two is about empathy, togetherness, and most likely a series of eureka moments where you will from time to time think 'I know exactly what you're talking about' and 'I felt that way, too'.

The five stages are Denial, Anger, Negotiation, Depression, and Acceptance. My belief is that they all play a role in how we process grief, and we don't need to worry about the fact that we experience each of these stages. in Part Three, we will explore some techniques and resources that can be employed should you get stuck in any of these stages (apart, of course, from Acceptance). I was fortunate in that I did not get stuck for too long in any of these stages, and in fact learned a lot about myself as I went on my journey. Lessons that I am grateful for, and which have enriched my life.

My hope is that you, too, can embrace the natural process of grief without letting it hold you back from the future that you deserve. Whether you have also experienced the traumatic loss of both of your parents, any other loved ones, whether you are recently separated or divorced, been made redundant, suffered the loss of a business, bankruptcy, insolvency, falling out with a friend, even moving house and relocating to a different area. All of these circumstances involve change. Even those where we have made a choice can leave us grieving for the certainty of what we leave behind. This grieving process can be hard to accept. By understanding how universally challenging this process is, I hope you can feel that you are not alone and are among many who share similar fears and anxieties to you.

The good news is that, as we have already discussed, you can use this as an opportunity to grow, and there is help at hand if you feel that you are stuck and unable to move forward.

Stage 1

Denial

I can understand why Denial has its place in the Kubler Ross grief cycle. When traumatic grief descends unexpectedly upon you, it is perfectly normal to periodically take a reflective breath and step back to pose the question, 'Did that just really happen?' These events that aren't supposed to happen to us, and only happen to other people, can make us feel like we are living on a movie set. I suspect that this is a coping mechanism employed by our neurology to protect us from shock. When I look back, I sometimes feel like I am watching events unfold at the cinema, or perhaps as if I was experiencing Astral Projection looking down as an objective third party and monitoring the situation from afar. I can see how this could be helpful from a neuroscientific perspective. A degree of dissociation to protect us from the horror of the circumstances. So, if this is Denial, then I definitely experienced it. Not, however, in the traditional sense.

I never felt like I was in denial of what happened. At no point did I kid myself that Mum and Dad hadn't died. I was cruelly and acutely aware of the harsh reality; I could not escape it. Denial possibly manifested itself in the form of cortisol and adrenaline. When I reflect and sit in wonder at how I managed to function, work, exercise, and deal with life so soon after losing my parents, then perhaps this is a form of denial. Again, as a defence mechanism, these two chemicals enabled me to function at some sort of level whilst partially anaesthetising me from the severity and magnitude of the situation. Of course, this is not sustainable, which is why every now and then I would shock myself with disbelief, suddenly remembering that my life had changed forever, and that what happened was indeed a very big deal.

My sense of perspective was maintained primarily by my brother Conal, who in the run-up to Mum and Dad's deaths, managed my expectations in his capacity as my older brother and also in his capacity as a doctor. There is something particularly haunting about a situation's capacity to gradually and then very rapidly progress from a minor deviation from life's traditional trajectory to your entire world falling apart right in front of your eyes. This, of course, was the essence of the pandemic. Look how we all became used to adjusting our lifestyle to accommodate a global catastrophe. Maybe the fact that it was global helped the world to adjust; everyone was, after all, in the same boat.

The haunting and sinister manner in which the tragic set of circumstances evolved felt like a 'Creeping Death'. The fact that I cannot pinpoint with any degree of accuracy the precise moment when the penny dropped that my life was about to change permanently and forever, I find somewhat stark.

Again, the cortisol and adrenaline would have played a significant part here, helping my mind and body to rationalise the inevitable wave of Post Traumatic Stress Disorder that was slowly taking its hold on me.

Each of the five stages acts as a form of calibration, almost like a check-in point for us to pause and reflect upon where we are at any given moment. I regularly revisit Denial in the form of 'Wow, that really did happen, didn't it?' It tends to happen after an extended period of life feeling normal, and going about my daily business without thinking about what occurred. I think that perhaps my subconscious from time to time decides to remind me of what happened, and I guess sometimes it still takes me by surprise.

Stage 2

Anger

Anger, for me, was my default position, and the stage of the grief cycle that I most easily and naturally headed towards when I was feeling at my most vulnerable. It provides the quickest and strongest adrenaline kick, and I know how to achieve it really easily. Just because it's easy to achieve, though, doesn't mean that it's necessarily a good idea. Anger has its place in terms of being useful, but in my opinion only when it's for a brief period leading to a moment of clarity, or to a period of extended peace. Peace, however, was not at the forefront of my mind when I was experiencing anger, and the purpose of this chapter to is to acknowledge how natural it is to feel anger when something grossly unjust and gruesome happens to you. But getting stuck in anger is not useful or healthy, and this is why Part 3 of this book exists. Anger is such a broad subject that I have split it into several sections, as follows:

Covid Deniers and Anti-Vaxxers

I have never ever felt rage and fury to the extent that I did when, soon after Mum and Dad's deaths, I began to notice the emergence of those who denied that Covid either existed, or believed that its ferocity had been exaggerated. And then, of course, there are those who refuse to take vaccines and wear masks, believing that lockdowns are an affront to their human rights.

Sometimes in life we get consumed with anger, perhaps if we feel that we have been betrayed, let down, or poorly treated. In many of these instances there are grey areas, doubts perhaps that we are being 100% objective in the way that we feel. That in itself can be uncomfortable, as guilt, shame, and confusion can emulsify with the anger to create a toxic brew of emotions. This in turn can cause values conflicts, cognitive dissonance, and uncertainty about which direction to take and the next appropriate course of action.

In my situation, this was absolutely not the case. What I experienced was pure unadulterated rage. My steely-eyed determination and courage removed any doubt or fear that I was potentially overreacting. Of course, social media played the strongest role in stoking the flames of my anger. There are two people among my business connections who became the focal point of my anger. I became so upset at the hypocrisy of these two individuals, who ironically participate in the coaching and holistic wellbeing industries, that they could be so cruel, insensitive, ignorant, arrogant, obnoxious, and entitled. Their social media pages were awash with mocking commentary of those 'sheeple' who were too thick and lazy to follow anything but the 'mainstream media' for their sources of information. Of course, we were all encouraged to access the dark web and 'do the research' to pave our way to enlightenment. They spread lies and misinformation about Covid-19, suggesting that it was a hoax, that it was part of a global conspiracy to control the masses and restrict our freedoms.

As I delved a little deeper, I stumbled across the most toxic community of Covid deniers, who had abandoned their compassion for people like me because I was an inconvenient paradigm that contradicted their deeply held beliefs. It was at this point that they showed their true colours, with commentary such as:

- 'But your parents were old; old people die, it's a fact of life; get over it'
- 'But did your parents have any underlying health conditions?'
- 'How do you know that the hospital didn't deliberately fake your parents' death certificates?'
- 'Are you sure it wasn't just flu?'
- 'You can't trust the medical staff, doctors or nurses, as they are all in on it'
- 'It's clear that you have been brainwashed, so you're hardly capable of thinking objectively'

This is what I encountered when I politely challenged any of these keyboard warriors. Going back to the two 'friends' that I mentioned. They also had a following, mainly from the holistic health community, and all of whom knew me – and knew me well. I am quite well known in the Essex business networking community, and as a consequence I am friends with many of these people on Facebook. Not one of them, nobody from that coven of lies, ever sent me a message, called me, checked in on me, and none of them certainly ever offered their condolences to me, as that would have acknowledged that Covid existed – and that was just too much for them. Frankly, I was fucking furious with them and had to 'unfollow' them so that I stopped seeing their propaganda intoxicating my newsfeed. It would have been impossible not to have been aware of what had happened; it was all over social media, and the influx of love and compassion from the majority of the people that I knew was heartening. I was bloody angry, though, about these others.

One of them was even so cruel as to send me a video of a holistic therapist talking about how traumatic it had been for her to be asked by the security guard at Morrisons to put a face mask on before she entered the store. She went on to court sympathy from her lunatic following by going on to explain how violated she felt when they refused her entry after she explained to them that she felt that masks weren't necessary to protect her against a virus that doesn't exist. I maintained my dignity with all of the people that I knew who were spreading this nonsense about, because I didn't have the time or energy to waste on them. I had already written them off, so there was no point in trying to engage them in a sensible discussion. They had gone too far. I had to learn to control my anger so that it didn't absorb me, but it was bloody hard to do this. Can you imagine how fucking livid I was listening to that stupid woman bleat on about her freedom when I had just lost my precious mum and dad? They would have loved to have had the opportunity to wear a mask and go food shopping. They can't do that, however, because they are dead, and they aren't coming back.

It's really hard not to take these affronts personally, particularly when the perpetrators know you, and know you well. Fortunately, I have sufficient perspective and foresight to understand and appreciate that it is not in my best interests to perpetuate a long-term campaign of rage against these idiots, and that their woefully unpleasant behaviour speaks volumes for them in terms of their values. I can reflect upon my lowest ebb during this period now with a degree of humour. Soon after Dad died, I ended up having a full-blown argument online (obviously) at 3am with a hairdresser from Oklahoma (I know!), following an evening spent with a bottle of vodka. She insisted that the virus was a hoax and that I had been misled by the hospital staff (including my brother), and that their death certificates had been faked. I'm not proud of how I responded, but it was not very nice at all, and the next morning I promptly deleted my comments. The majority of these people are disenfranchised with traditional life and have an axe to grind with the establishment. Their paranoia around government institutions and the media has blinded them and inoculated them from compassion. Under normal circumstances, this wouldn't bother me. For instance, if somebody wants to believe that the earth is flat, then let them get on with it. It's not going to hurt anyone, other perhaps than their children's chances of succeeding in school at physics and geography.

On the other hand, spreading dangerous misinformation about Covid vaccines, and nonsense about how they change our DNA, is downright irresponsible and, in my view, should be illegal. How many vulnerable and impressionable members of our community have died as a result of listening to toxic propaganda from those in a position of trust? I'll give you an example: a holistic therapist welcomes an elderly client into their treatment room to perform Reiki, or an aromatherapy massage. The therapist spends the 45-minute session warning the client against taking the vaccine, citing any number of falsehoods, and putting the fear of God into this poor person. The client subsequently decides not to take the vaccine, catches Covid, and dies a few weeks later. The only question that you have to ask yourself in this instance is if there was a proven audit trail that could demonstrate this sequence of events. And if this client was your mother, would you or would you not want that therapist prosecuted for manslaughter?

Awareness of Anger, Acceptance, and Management

I used anger as a calibration tool, subconsciously to create a more resourceful state of focus and clarity. That was my secondary gain. Thankfully, I became quickly aware of this, which gave me the choice to accept my anger and then manage it. It wasn't a steady journey out of anger, as I regularly stepped back into it in order to change my emotional state. Left unchecked, this habit could have become incredibly damaging. Without awareness, the addiction to rage in an attempt to stimulate an adrenaline rush would undoubtedly have caused long-term health issues, both physically and mentally. Adrenaline and cortisol have their place, but left to run riot they become the chemicals of toxic stress, increasing our chances of heart attack, stroke, and even cancer. I did, however, learn from anger; I learned that from anger comes clarity, once the red mist dissipates. This is why I am now 100% clear about what I want out of life, and 100% clear about what I *don't* want out of life. The tragedy of what happened is so powerful an anchor that it is easy for me to have the courage to stick resolutely to my principles.

Anger with Family and Friends

You take it out on those closest to you. When you have that amount of rage inside you, with so many unanswered questions, trying to make sense out of a situation that defies logic, it keeps you in a state of high alert. All it takes is for someone to say the wrong thing in the wrong way, using the wrong tone of voice, and all tolerance evaporates in the blink of an eye. Any good, supportive friend will understand this and remain consistent and constant in their support for you, standing by your side throughout.

My advice to those of you who are suffering in grief is to be crystal clear to your loved ones about what you want and need from them. Please don't leave it to chance. Some people are incredibly intuitive about the needs of their loved ones, and will instinctively know what to say or do, or perhaps more importantly will know what *not* to say or do. Others, frankly, are pretty clueless and will fumble around like a bull in a china shop, almost always saying something that will act as a trigger to you. Please help them by telling them what you need from them.

If people make mistakes and upset you, remember that it is highly unlikely that there has been any malice or sinister intent behind any clumsy dialogue. Many people are nervous about what to say about death, and as we all know, nerves don't always bring out the best in us in terms of our ability to communicate with any degree of elegance or panache.

You do sometimes hear stories of couples who split up after one of them suffers a loss. After experiencing something so tragic, it would be an awful shame if you then had to deal with the grief of a relationship that went into freefall. If the relationship was already in decline, then that of course is a different story; perhaps the traumatic event was the straw that broke the camel's back. I was very fortunate that our tragic events galvanised my closest relationships even more. I am closer now to my husband Ian and my brother Conal than I have ever been, and I am so, so grateful for that. We were already close, but now it feels like we are under some kind of divine instruction from Mum and Dad.

Anger at Everyday Occurrences

I thought that I would close this chapter with a brief reflection upon how mundane everyday occurrences can act as triggers for grief-related anger. I wanted to provide reassurance that it was completely normal and nothing to worry about. The subconscious, when we are feeling vulnerable, actively seeks out evidence to reinforce its belief structure. When we are feeling particularly alert to our grief situations, which we might otherwise ignore or react to with indifference or even humour, can cause us to erupt. As long as this doesn't happen as a continuous loop, then we don't need to be too concerned about it.

Here are some examples of when I became disproportionately angry:

- At times, I became resentful of my businesses and work, particularly if faced with what I regarded to be irrelevant challenges

- On the anniversary of Mum's death, two clients emailed me to advise that they had decided to use another company for their services
- At times, I became resentful and irritated by minor inconveniences
- People on TV annoyed me more than usual
- I was taking things far more personally than I normally would
- I reacted far more aggressively when a property developer that we were dealing with decided not to pay us a large amount of money that they owed us

In some of these circumstances, anger was a helpful tool to precipitate positive action to remedy an unpleasant situation, but in many circumstances my reaction was overkill. As I said, it didn't last forever, so I wasn't overly concerned by it, and now I am completely back to my normal self. The final part of this book will offer some tools to assist should you feel that you are stuck in anger, which we have already said is not a healthy place to remain.

Stage 3

Negotiation

In this stage of the grief cycle, it centres on the hope that we can avoid a cause of grief. Ordinarily, the negotiation for the life of a loved one to continue is made in exchange for perhaps a reformed lifestyle. Sometimes we might bargain or compromise, playing a game of mental tennis in our heads. You might have heard of scenarios where in desperate times people have 'negotiated with God' and offered to 'trade their life for mine'.

I think that, regardless of whether you are religious or not, it is quite natural to flirt with this stage. When you reach the point of desperation, you'll try pretty much anything to save the lives of your family, so why not throw the kitchen sink at it? Playing games in your head can make you feel like you've got a choice, and that by appealing to a higher power or the universe you can enhance the prospects of your loved one, even if it's by the tiniest percentage. It is, of course, a superstition, but many of us do it. I still avoid the cracks in the pavement and play silly OCD games in my head with obsessive counting. All that we are doing when we do this is playing a game of probability. When life is stressful and we begin to feel out of control, superstition can play a soothing role. Like all of the stages, it is fine in small doses, but when it spirals out of control then it is time to seek a little assistance.

A good example of this perhaps is when driving to work you say to yourself that if you get past the next set of traffic lights without them turning red it means that you're going to close the deal at your next sales meeting. Again, a perfectly natural game that we sometimes play in our heads. Negotiation and bargaining with the lives of our loved ones is understandable and natural.

So, with all of this in mind, it may come to surprise you that I didn't really experience this. In the run up to Mum and Dad's deaths, I didn't negotiate at all. Did I pray for them? Yes, of course I did. I am privately religious, and prayed that they would both survive, prayed that they would have the strength to recover once they survived, and prayed that we as a family would have the strength to get through this whole nightmare so that we could support one another. I didn't, however, offer to trade lives or make outlandish promises about being a changed person. I was too focused on attending to the reality of what was going on each day, and I just didn't feel that superstition had any significant role to play in supporting me through this journey.

After they died, I did for a short while start to play some 'What if' games in my head. I wondered if it would have made any difference had Mum's previous attempts to have surgery been successful, and whether she would have recovered and come home before the virus had infected the hospital. This, of course, would then have saved Dad. I then wondered if the care support staff, who would have come in each day to help Dad look after Mum, might have brought the virus in with them. I tried to calculate the probability of survival in that instance. Would surgery a week before have helped, or should it have been 10 days, 14 days, or would we have needed a clear month to be 'belt and braces' safe? Fortunately, this game of probability didn't last long, and only surfaces from time to time whilst chatting to my brother.

Once again, I feel that this is one way that our brains process tragic and extreme circumstances. It is a form of calibrating, trying to make sense and rationalising our thoughts before making a decision about how we are going to feel or what we are going to do next. As humans, we crave a degree of certainty, and our decision-making systems rely to an extent upon having a degree of logic upon which we can justify our next thought or action. The more bizarre and horrific the circumstance, the more challenging this is to achieve with any degree of panache.

Stage 4

Depression

Perhaps the most challenging phase of the grief cycle for me was depression. At least with anger, you can sometimes channel it to create a more positive outcome, or utilise it as an intermediate or gateway emotion. Whilst depression can also offer moments of clarity, it is a deeply unpleasant place to reside. When stress becomes toxic, it triggers anxiety. When anxiety takes hold of you for long enough, it can take you down a rabbit hole of hopelessness that can ultimately lead to depression.

Thankfully, I didn't get stuck in depression, or indeed in any of the other phases of the grief cycle. I certainly teetered on the edge of getting stuck, but when I did, I employed a multitude of strategies outlined later in the book, and on each and every occasion I got myself back on track.

For me, depression manifested itself in prolonged periods of deep sadness. After the funeral and perhaps up to six months later, I began to feel an intense sense of loneliness. I was insanely busy at work, and business was thankfully going well. I was utterly convinced that 'everyone' thought that because I was thriving everything was fine, and that I had 'got over it' and 'moved on'. I hadn't got over it all, and whilst I had moved forward, I had not moved on. I still haven't got over it, and I probably never will. And you know what? That's okay; I'm fine with that. The reason that it's okay for me to continue to grieve is because it feels disingenuous not to. Grief, after all, is love manifesting itself in a different way.

It's difficult for those around you to understand this. Some people have an inherent desire to try and 'fix' you, or provide a solution. That's not what I wanted, and I found that this compounded my depression. This depressive state didn't stop me from making progress in my life; far from it. It did, however, make me a little paranoid and prone to bouts of 'mind reading' that were sometimes very accurate, but on other occasions not so much. For instance, I was convinced that as a period of time had elapsed since Mum and Dad died, most of my friends felt that I should by now have 'moved on and got over it'. I had little evidence that this was the case, but I believed it – and believed it strongly. I felt that nobody wanted me to talk about my parents, when that is all that I wanted to talk about. In fact, it is still what I want to talk about to this day. Ironically, as a result of this belief, I found myself not speaking about them, and this only served to compound my depression.

Mum and Dad and their home represented the ultimate security and safety for me. No matter what happened throughout my life, I always knew that I could go to their house and there would be a meal on the table and a bed to sleep in for as long as I needed or wanted to. It was my safe zone, and I knew everything was going to be okay whilst I was there. The sad reality that this was gone forever made me feel so desperately unhappy. I couldn't tell you the number of times that I would grab my phone and call their landline number, but it was a lot. I still do it now from time to time. If something exciting had happened, I would always want to share that with Mum and Dad. I would call Dad to discuss the football results on a Saturday and Sunday afternoon. He supported Arsenal and I support Liverpool, so there was always plenty to discuss, particularly when our teams played each other. They loved to hear all about what was going on in my and Ian's lives, always hoping to hear encouraging news about work, business, and our friends. Thankfully, in recent years, there had been mostly positive news to share. Equally though, if I was feeling down or unresourceful, I knew that a phone call with Mum or Dad would instantly make me feel so much better. They just knew instinctively what to say and how to say it to make me feel good. I was so, so unbelievably upset that I had lost that forever. I felt like my support network had shrunk, and that made me feel vulnerable and exposed.

These thoughts tended to surface either first thing in the morning or late at night. Funnily enough, during the day I was too busy for these feelings to dominate for any sustainable period. And thankfully, I did not get stuck here. I've never taken medication for depression or anxiety in my life, although it would have been perfectly acceptable for me to have done so at that point – and indeed at some other periods of my life in my younger years when I struggled with my mental health. I am most fortunate to have been trained by some of the world's most talented mindset coaches, so I have the tools at my disposal to tunnel myself out of the deepest and darkest of holes. I would never dismiss medication, though, and would urge any of you to seek professional medical help should you feel that you need some extra support. I know many people who lead happy and fully functional lives whilst being supported by a combination of medication and therapy. I am sharing my experience, and I count myself lucky to have found my own way through.

Stage 5

Acceptance

I am writing this chapter a little over a year after Mum and Dad's funeral. I have spent 12 months darting from one stage of the grief cycle to the other. From Anger to Negotiation to Depression to Denial to Acceptance. And then back to Depression, before reverting to Anger again, and so on and so forth. It's an unpredictable rollercoaster, made all the more challenging by the fact that we are still, as I write, living in a pandemic. I still have yet to hug my friends and extended family. I am constantly reminded about the cause of my parents' deaths, and it is impossible to ignore it. However, somehow finally now I feel like I am in pretty good shape. I am fit, healthy, happy, and thriving in pretty much every area of my life. The reason for this is that I have embraced Post Traumatic Growth and am now navigating my life through an extended period of Acceptance.

On the face of it, Acceptance feels like the opposite of the Denial stage. I thought about this long and hard, and upon reflection it is now clear to me that, like Denial, Acceptance is an experience which occurs both consciously and subconsciously. I had accepted Mum and Dad's deaths as soon as they happened. I was in no doubt that they had gone, because I had been so close to the situation that I would have been totally delusional to have thought otherwise. On a subconscious level, though, I had not accepted anything. I was so drastically upset, angry, stunned, shocked, lost, and afraid, whilst feeling like I was living in a parallel universe, that the word acceptance was anathema to me.

Now, however, whilst all of those emotions and sensations still feel very much alive for me as memories, I am graduating sustainably towards core states of peace, calm, wholeness, oneness, and love. The sense of empowerment that has remained with me throughout the whole process is now far more aligned with my values, as it is no longer fueled by anger. The fuel of anger can only sustain itself for so long before it ravages the soul and leaves it fatigued and war-weary. Instead, my optimism for the future, my courage to move my life forward in a way that works for me and my family, empowers me. I feel grounded, confident, focused, motivated, compassionate, and excited. All of those values, characteristics, and emotions were always there, and finally I have given myself permission to open my heart to let them surface. I guess I just needed time to navigate the five stages of grief with a little help from my personal development toolkit, so that I could acclimatise, adjust, and calibrate my emotions until I felt comfortable to move forward. I don't have any regrets, and I trust that my subconscious was always going to lead me to where I need to be.

I can identify a number of events, milestones, and actions that, no matter how small, appear as evidence of the longevity of my acceptance. Conal and I are permitted to place a permanent headstone at Mum and Dad's grave now that it has had a full year to settle. Having agreed upon our choice of headstone and the wording, we can now look forward to that arriving and replacing the modest wooden cross that stands there, loyally and proudly marking where Mum and Dad have been laid to rest. We donated the majority of our parents' clothes to charity, which felt like a good thing to do. We did, however, keep hold of a number of items that really reminded us of them. I sent them off to a keepsake company that transformed their clothes into memory cushions and teddy bears. I now have a cushion for Dad, made from the shirt that he wore on the day that he went into hospital, and a cushion for Mum, made from my favourite jumper of hers. They take pride of place in our home, and I look forward to sharing the others – which are now on order – with Conal and his family.

We are planning a memorial service to be held at Brentwood Cathedral in April 2022. This will mark the two-year anniversary of my parents' deaths. Originally, we had intended to hold this event in October 2020, by which time we optimistically thought that the virus would have fizzled out. We then delayed until April 2021, and July 2021, before deciding to put sufficient time in place for us to confidently set a date. Whilst initially it was disappointing to have such a long wait to host the memorial service, we now view it in a slightly different way. Whilst I am not entirely sure that the expression 'time heals' is appropriate in this instance (I prefer 'time makes you resilient'), the temporal gap has for us meant that we can look forward to the memorial service as more of a celebration of our parents' lives, reminiscing about old times, and reflecting with humour on a whole number of past events and occasions. Had the service taken place immediately after the tragic events, I'm sure it would have been incredibly moving, but I suspect there would have been more of a sombre tone to the event. Conal and I are now looking forward to the service and the wake that will follow. It will be an opportunity for us to meet up with so many family and friends who loved Mum and Dad. We haven't seen many of these people for a number of years, purely through circumstance, and there are a great many who would have been supporting us with their physical presence during our period of intense grief but were prevented from doing so due to Covid restrictions, who we will also be longing to see – perhaps for the first time in over two years.

Ian and I have decided to renovate Mum and Dad's house in Brentwood, and move into it, making it our forever family home. This feels like it will bring everything full circle. This was my and Conal's family home growing up, and now Ian and I have a chance to transform it into our dream home, whilst preserving the most precious childhood memories. Conal can then visit with his wife and children to enjoy the house where they spent time with Mum and Dad. It just feels right and the obvious thing to do, almost destined by fate.

As you can see, we are looking forward with optimism, hope, and love, whilst remaining connected to our wonderful memories of Mum and Dad. This is what Acceptance looks like to me. Acceptance is not giving up and settling for second best. It is learning to be at peace with a situation that is beyond your control. It is understanding that whilst there are events that you cannot control, you can determine how you respond to those events. It is working out for yourself how you can bounce forward from tragedy, empowered, courageous, and having evaporated fears and anxieties that have plagued you for decades. It is the reality that, having experienced the darkest and most brutal sequence of events, you have grown in compassion whilst developing the most intense self-belief. It is the dawning within your consciousness that everything that you do from now on is a reflection of the love that you have for those that you have lost. You can strive forward with the most liberating sense of confidence, smiling with pride, as you are reminded that you continue to grow as a person, motivated by the approving love and smiles of your lost loved ones watching over you.

Just stop for a moment to think and reflect at the power of that. For me, there is no greater anchor than the thought of Mum and Dad proudly keeping an eye on what I am doing. Dad grinning and not saying a huge amount, and Mum's curiosity prompting a volley of questions about whatever project I happen to be involved in at the time. Just because they are no longer here in the physical sense does not mean that they aren't aware from a spiritual perspective. I can sense their presence, I can feel their love, and I can hear them gently encouraging me to seize the day and to elicit the joy from every second of every minute of every day for the rest of my life.

I have received my instructions, and I gratefully accept them.

Part Three – Introduction

At times, I reflect on what happened and wonder how I am still here, and how I got to where I am on this day. It can feel sometimes like I have ridden on the crest of a wave, somehow managing to keep myself afloat but not really understanding how and why that happened. Reflection, however, is a most helpful device, as it encourages us to pause, take a breath, and allow our subconscious to gently filter epiphanies to us that help us to make sense of the most enigmatic periods of our lives.

The good news is that all of us already have the resources within us to navigate our lives through even the most challenging episodes. Sometimes it takes the most traumatic and dramatic turn of events to elicit our innermost power and genius, and depending upon how much practice we have had, this will either happen quickly and efficiently or excruciatingly slowly.

The purpose of this section of the book is to share with you some resources, practices, habits, and exercises that helped me to take control of my life. Everything that I go on to mention helped me in some way to navigate my journey from tragedy to empowerment. However, we are all different, and some strategies will work better for some people than others. So what I am offering you here are not rules, but tools that you can have at your disposal to utilise as you see fit. Sometimes just knowing that you have a range of tools designed to help you travel through choppy waters can be enough on its own. My attitude is that forewarned is forearmed, and everything that I refer to can be used for a whole range of healthy and positive outcomes.

The Basics

Nature and The Great Outdoors

There is something very grounding about taking a walk among nature. It has a way of making us feel insignificant; not in a bad way, but by providing a sense of perspective. For me, it's how I imagine it would be like to be watching Earth from a space station, marvelling at how incredible the planet is, but also how trivial and insignificant each individual event is. When I walk in the countryside, come rain or shine, I am reminded that nature, the climate, and seasons, continue to function come what may. I find this incredibly grounding, and a foundation for my gratitude. As I type this chapter, it is 6am, and as I stare out of my lounge window into the back garden, I notice the grey overcast sky. But as I become aware of the gentle breeze causing the lower branches of our willow tree to sway, I feel a sense of calm.

When the whole world comes crashing down around you, taking time out each day for yourself is essential. Even if you live in a city, the chances are there will be a park or path by a river that will offer you some solace. Pay attention to your senses as you notice the trees, plants, bushes, and flowers. What can you see? What can you smell? What can you taste? Is it the humidity of the moist air on your tongue, or the scent of freshly cut grass? What can you hear? Birdsong? If so, how many different birds are vying for your attention? What can you feel? Are you walking on grass, mud, or gravel? How does that feel on your feet?

You can enjoy this time alone or with a friend, maybe both. If you have a dog, this can be a wonderful time to enjoy nature with a pet that loves you unconditionally. Over time, perhaps you might wish to explore different walking routes. Some of them might be on your doorstep; others might require a short drive, maybe more achievable at the weekends if you are busy midweek. Even as I type this section of the chapter, I feel calm, as I temporarily forget about everything else that I have to do today and cast my gaze back out to the willow tree with its leaves gently stirring. I'll head out in a moment and walk my dog Toby for half an hour. I've got a choice of three routes from my house, and I'll only decide when I set foot out of the house – and not a moment before.

Physical Exercise

The benefits to our mental health of taking regular physical exercise are profoundly obvious. When Mum and Dad died, I took to running to help me remain grounded, and also to maintain my physical fitness. The gyms were closed, as we were in lockdown, so we were limited in terms of what we could do. Fortunately, where we live there are a number of beautiful jogging routes that I enjoy, regardless of whether I am running 5 or 10 kilometres. I was also fortunate that the spring and summer of 2020 were the hottest and brightest in recent history. It made getting up to go for a run so much easier than if it had been raining every morning (a bit like the following year so far).

That said, I was also aware that I was suffering with pretty bad fatigue. I previously got up each morning at 5am, and was off and out half an hour later. I was now getting up at 6:30am to 7am, and taking at least an hour to get myself into a state where I could do anything productive. This, of course, was and is fine. I didn't push myself, and I acknowledged and accepted that it was going to be a gradual process, and my body probably would not have thanked me had I pushed myself into training for an Iron Man triathlon a fortnight or so after the funeral. Physical exercise was there to serve me, and not the other way around. If all I could muster on a day where I felt particularly tired was a walk among nature, as I mention above, then that would be fine.

On other days, though, I might feel a burst of energy. This could then lead to a 5k, or maybe even a 10k run if I was feeling particularly energetic. And this rhythm of regular exercise made me feel like I was achieving something, regardless of whatever else was going on in my world. Already, I think you can see a pattern. Not only is exercise good for our physical and mental health; it is also like a walk among nature, a gesture of kindness back towards ourselves. During moments of intense grief, it is incredibly important that we communicate kindly towards ourselves, and taking time out of our normal busy and hectic lifestyles is one such way to do just that.

So, I am not saying that you need to sign up with a personal trainer the day after your loved one dies – although, if the thought of that excites you, then absolutely why not? What I am saying is that exercise can play a role in helping you to claw back some normality in your life, and to help you to remain physically and mentally in a space where you can feel resilient enough to deal with all the phone calls and emails from family, friends, solicitors, financial advisers, etc. It's about putting some foundations in place that work for you.

Healthy Nutrition

Okay, so with this one there is an element of 'Do as I say, not as I did'. I told you at the start that I would be honest with you, and I will be. After my parents died, I made a pact with myself that I would eat and drink whatever I wanted for a year, before reverting to a lifestyle of moderation and health.

Now don't get me wrong, I wasn't in any way reckless, but it would be fair to say that during the week I ate healthily and didn't drink, and come the weekend I would relax, enjoy eating takeaways, crisps, chocolate, and sweets, and drank alcohol as I saw fit and felt like it. Fortunately, I have sufficient self-awareness to recognise if I am going too far with eating and drinking, and I also have my husband Ian living with me to help me regulate my intake. He does most of the cooking, so that helped to keep our diets healthy. I also have the benefit of an older brother who is a doctor. If my weight was starting to creep up, Conal would make gentle references to type 2 Diabetes and remind me not to get too carried away.

As with exercise and nature, healthy nutrition is another way with which you can express kindness to yourself. Strike a balance and give serious thought before you embark upon a punishing change to your diet. A year later, I have found my rhythm with my diet and have lost almost two stone in weight, having pretty much cut sugar and processed foods from my diet. I have reset my relationship with alcohol so that I drink in order to celebrate rather than to simply acknowledge the fact that it is, for example, Thursday. I feel happier, more energetic, and more in control now than I have ever done before in my life, and much of this is down to how I eat and drink. I can still take a day off and enjoy a treat day if I am celebrating a friend's birthday in a restaurant, and I can do that now without guilt, and safe in the knowledge that I am still 'on plan'.

Over time, perhaps give some thought to what might work best for you. Experiment and consider what foods you enjoy that make you feel good, not just at the time of eating but for hours afterwards. Use your intuition and do some research, speak to friends, and consider whether you wish to consult a nutritional therapist to help you seek out equilibrium.

Sleep

A good night's sleep is, and has always been for me, a necessary component for having a great day. If I suffer a broken night of sleep, the next day begins on the back foot. I used to get by on five hours' sleep per night, and probably to an extent wore it like a badge of honour. Interestingly, there were segments of the personal development world that championed getting by on four hours' sleep, supported by a vegan diet, affording us all more time to achieve everything on our personal and professional bucket lists. In recent years, however, I am seeing much more advice focusing on the importance of us all getting between seven and eight hours' sleep per night.

It makes sense to me, and more so during a period of grief. I suffered extreme fatigue in the months that followed, and I would say for up to a year afterwards. This was not the time to force myself to get up at 5am and bounce around like a spring lamb. So, I listened to my body and mind, went to bed when I was tired, and got up when I felt like I had slept sufficiently to have recouped the energy to face the responsibilities that lay ahead of me.

The more I read about sleep, the more I appreciate how important it is for our immune system, and for our body and mind to recover, recharge, refresh, and regenerate overnight. Sleep helps us fight infection, regulates our blood pressure, and helps us to manage our weight. The quality of our decision-making and our moods is affected by sleep. It is worth spending time working out a sleep hygiene pattern that works for you. For me, it is going to bed at 10pm and getting up at 5:30am. I try to avoid social media and emails in the hour before bedtime, and I would like to avoid all forms of digital stimulation in the hour before bedtime. I imagine that I would be more rested if I did. When I wake up, I no longer immediately check my phone to read the news, emails, or social media. This means that I have a gentler start to the day.

Give some thought to the temperature of your bedroom, whether noise or the absence of noise is helpful to you, the quality of your bed, pillows, and mattress; even how much light you like to have in your bedroom. Experiment to find out what works best for you. We spend so much time of our lives asleep that it is worth investing some time and energy to ensure that you give yourself the best chance of making the most of that time.

Simple Strategies

Breathing Exercises

This may sound obvious, but paying attention to how we breathe can make a radical difference to how we manage our mental and physical state. There are various breathing exercises that work in slightly different ways. If you are interested, you can find out all about them with a simple Google search. To keep things nice and simple, though, I am going to encourage you to stick to a simple routine which works well when we feel overwhelmed, anxious, and when flashbacks of our trauma descend upon us. Simply inhale through your nose for 4 seconds, and exhale out of your mouth for 4 seconds. Repeat this pattern 5 times, and you will notice that you begin to feel more relaxed and less afraid. Like many of these strategies, this one can be used on a daily basis as a preventative measure, and not only when we wish to calm ourselves down. With regular practice and repetition, our nervous system can and does develop to encourage a more consistently healthy sense of wellbeing. The opposite, of course, is also true, so it's important to take stock from time to time of how much self-care we are adopting.

Mindfulness

This is a word that has surfaced in the mainstream media in recent years, which is great news. Schools are introducing mindfulness classes to assist the management of mental health issues amongst children and young adults. But what is mindfulness? For me, it was giving myself an opportunity to pause, even for a brief moment, and forget what I was doing or thinking about beforehand, and not giving thought to what I had to do next. The great thing about mindfulness is that it can be done anywhere, and nobody around you is even aware that you are doing it. Next time you eat a meal, switch off the television and turn your phone upside down, so you're not tempted to check it. Take some time to think about what you are eating, the taste of your food, the texture. Enjoy eating it slowly, maybe giving some thought about how the food ended up in front of you. What was its journey? This, for me, gives rise to a sense of gratitude about the food that I am enjoying and that is sustaining me.

You can be mindful as you look out of your window at home or in the office. Even sitting down in your living room, you can stop and scan the room, noticing things that you haven't observed for months or even years, such as a book or CD on a shelf that inspires a sense of nostalgia. Mindfulness is grounding, and is a useful strategy to overcome anxiety and overwhelm, which are common reactions to grief. My favourite technique for mindfulness is to spend ten minutes or so paying attention to each of the five senses. I will seek out three things that I can see, hear, feel, taste and smell. As you focus on carrying out this task, it distracts you from the previous feelings of despair, fear or stress. It is such a powerful tool, because it reminds us that the world has not stopped turning just because we had the audacity to pause for ten minutes and reflect and marvel at our natural environment.

Meditation

I have been meditating on a daily basis each morning for years. Before I check my phone for emails or my social media, I spend between five and ten minutes meditating. I have several meditation apps on my phone that I use if I feel like using a guided meditation, or alternatively I have memorised some simple meditation routines that work effectively for me. The benefit of meditation for me is setting my intention for the day by grounding myself. Again, like many of these strategies, it is a gift and symbol of intent to care for myself. Not only does it have the immediate effect of making me feel calm and grounded, but the incremental benefit over an extended period of time is one of enhanced resilience and energy to fulfil the tasks of the coming day without feeling horrified at the extent of what lies ahead. With the right mindset, this task can feel exciting rather than frightening. I am, in fact, at my most resourceful when I also meditate at lunchtime for 5-10 minutes, and again before bedtime to maximise my chance of having a great night's sleep. Even a couple of minutes each day is enough to make a difference. Scientists have discovered that those of us who meditate on a regular basis experience a neurological shift. Our amygdala, which is the 'fight or flight' centre in our brains, shrinks after an extended period of mindfulness or meditation. Not only that, but the connections between the area that assist us with focus and concentration grow stronger. That's compelling evidence if ever I saw it that daily meditation is a sage investment of our time.

Gratitude Journal

Keeping a gratitude journal when your world is falling apart might seem challenging and unrealistic. In the days following my parents' deaths, gratitude was not high up on my agenda, and I probably would have reacted less than charitably had anyone – despite their good intentions – suggested that I start keeping a gratitude journal. As the weeks and months roll by, though, it is worth spending a few minutes each day keeping an eye on micro events that offer you some respite. These could be anything from receiving a WhatsApp message from an old university friend who you haven't spoken to in years, who has heard your sad news and messages you to tell you that they are thinking of you. It could be a smile from a stranger as they walk past you in the street, or your pet dog leaping into your lap to comfort you as they witness you once again descending into tears during an early morning meltdown. All of these and many more happened to me. And on days that I remember to keep a gratitude journal, I feel more robust and invigorated by the incredible sense of compassion that is all around us. Sometimes we need to be reminded we are loved and that there are many people around us who care about us, and that in general the world is a benign space inhabited by people who, on the whole, have their hearts in the right place.

From a neuroscience perspective, and without getting too geeky, when we focus our attention on things that we are grateful for, our brains seek out evidence to support this belief. This action then stimulates more neurotransmitters to the brain, particularly dopamine and serotonin, and this in turn creates feelings of contentment.

Set One Goal for the Day

Have you ever heard the expression that 'if you make your bed each and every day then you have achieved something within the first minute of getting up'? I think that this originates from the military in some way, shape, or form. And I believe it is great advice. If you start the day with a win, then the chances are that you will become perhaps a little addicted to achievements, and as the day progresses you then build upon that early win to achieve more and more. Don't worry about whether anyone else feels like it's a win – if it feels like a win to you, then that's all that matters. When we are working our way through grief, fulfilling even the simplest of tasks can feel like climbing a mountain. So, be kind to yourself and start off by focusing on one task per day to achieve, then you can build upon that gradually over time as you become stronger. It could be anything from going for a ten-minute walk, to putting the bins out for collection, or returning a phone call from a relative that called you a few weeks beforehand to check in on you.

Small Victory Celebrations

As you start to build momentum with your daily goals, it is imperative that you celebrate each and every win. I don't necessarily mean that you have to crack open the Dom Perignon every time you change your bed linen, but I do feel that it is a good idea to reflect at the end of each day upon your achievements – no matter how small they are. I would set myself micro goals, including replying to messages, keeping on top of my emails, dealing with some of Mum and Dad's admin, and then reward myself with a cup of tea or listening to some music, for instance, after each small victory. Keep on doing this for long enough and you'll instill some habits that will, if you so choose, generate a consistent degree of high performance. As I reflect back on the last year, I can pat myself on the back for progressing from arguing with strangers on the internet at 4am after drinking a bottle of vodka, to growing all four of our businesses to a level of record-breaking sales. Rome was not built in a day; it was built after a period of incremental change that was persistent, with many pauses for reflection and celebration.

Power Team

Who are your power team? By that I mean the five people that, if you broke down in the middle of the night in a dark country lane, would be the first you would call to help you get back home. When something dreadful happens, your friends want to help you, but they may not wish to intrude. It's up to us to give them permission to get stuck in and help us, and it's also up to us to be explicit about the type of help that we want and need – as well as the type of help that we *don't* want or need.

We need to spoon feed our friends with simple to follow instructions about how they can help us, so that they feel confident to step in when needed. By putting together your power team, you have a variety of people that love you and who you can check in with if you are feeling vulnerable. Create a WhatsApp group with all of them, and set the ground rules in advance of how you would like this to work. You may find that you don't use it very often, but as with many of these strategies, knowing that it is there is often enough. And if you do need to use it, then you've already set the intention with five mates who have already agreed to help you.

Specialist Strategies

Neurolinguistic Programming

I was introduced to NLP about 15 years ago, after I met a life coach called Gina Gardiner at a business networking event. At the time I was leading a reasonably happy life, but I was feeling a little unfulfilled on the relationship front. I was also finding business a little frustrating, and felt that I should have been making swifter progress towards my goals. Life was okay, but I suspected that something was missing. Fortunately, I have always been fascinated with human psychology, and had naturally gravitated to reading books about mindset and psychology, completely unprompted and without any external influence. This provoked a curiosity in me that has lasted a lifetime.

There is a presupposition in NLP that 'you get what you focus on', so it is no surprise upon reflection that I sought out more and more information on psychology and started to meet other people who shared a similar interest. Now in 2021, I have read hundreds of books and spent hours studying NLP, coaching, neuroscience, and hypnotherapy. I am blessed with a community of likeminded people who share a similar mindset, and we educate, mentor, and support each other throughout life's challenges, and celebrate all of the wonderful moments that we share together.

So, what actually is NLP? Neurolinguistic Programming offers us the tools to better understand how our brain processes the words that we use on a daily basis, and how that can influence our past, present, and future. It also offers us strategies that we can employ to observe human behaviour and elicit the aspects that benefit us and help us to achieve our goals. It enables us to 'think better' to develop and maintain perspective; it encourages us to clearly define our goals, to find someone who has already achieved something similar whilst empowering us to model their excellence so that we can enjoy similar success.

Over the years, I have studied NLP to the point where I have numerous accreditations, including becoming a Master Practitioner, Business Practitioner, and a licensed trainer in a specialist aspect of NLP called 'Identity by Design'. The impact on my business and personal life has been profound. The more I studied NLP and lived by its principles, the easier life became. For example, the quality of my relationships started to improve, both professionally and personally. I stopped taking things personally and became curious about other people's behaviour. Rather than jump to the most negative conclusion, I would aim to see things from other people's perspectives. It provided me with a sense of objectivity and neutrality that I had been subconsciously craving for most of my life. Slowly but surely, it helped me to start chipping away at the tension, aggression, anxiety, stress, and depression that had subtly, but persistently, handicapped me for most of my life.

As the years went by, my ability to deal with stressful situations improved dramatically. I started to work at cause and not effect. I abandoned the victim mentality that had form for rearing its head from time to time, and adopted and took responsibility for my life. If something happened that was less than helpful, I would look for the opportunity to grow or learn in some way shape or form. And this is how NLP played such a significant role in my response and reaction to Mum and Dad's deaths.

There were times following the tragedy when I struggled to make sense of what had happened; when I felt in complete and utter despair; and when I was finding it really difficult to imagine what the future might look like, having had half of my family wiped out in a global pandemic. In my younger days, I would have bottled up my thoughts and carried on regardless. But the cracks would have started to appear over time, with a decline in my mental health, and most likely a toxic dependency on alcohol and poor choice relationships. Thankfully, though, I asked for help when I needed it. My NLP community boasts a wealth of kind and capable practitioners, all of whom I could contact and would offer their help to me when I needed it the most. Sometimes I just needed someone to listen to me and not comment, but there were other occasions when I benefited from a sense of perspective. This happened a few times when my thought processes started to nosedive down a few toxic rabbit holes. This was completely natural, given how vulnerable I was feeling at the time. It was another NLP practitioner that took me through an NLP process that helped me to retain a healthier perspective on the situation, so that I could move forward and leave that particular frustration behind me. Another practitioner helped me to work out what my subconscious was craving, by taking me through a beautiful and gentle process called 'Core Transformation'. I learned that, as a result of my grief, I was craving love, inner peace, and connection, and this process gave me the tools to access those core states whenever I needed them. It is a truly wonderful process, and a gift to be able to access the process now whenever I need to.

In addition to these interventions, I also accessed a multitude of NLP techniques that I had learned over the years, and reintroduced them into my daily routine. For those of you unfamiliar with NLP, what this means is that I carried out a number of visualisation exercises to help me to imagine how good the future could be. I 'future paced' many scenarios where I could imagine being happy spending time with my family and friends, enjoying conversations and laughing about old times. This was such a useful tool for me at a time when I was restricted, as we all were, in terms of who we could physically meet up with.

The more I practised these visualisation exercises, the more resilient I became. This is due to something called Neuroplasticity. In the same way that toxic thought patterns can become engrained in our neurology, so thankfully can the opposite. So, remember my comment from earlier in this chapter that 'You get what you focus on'? This is why a pessimist can end up leading a life that becomes a self-fulfilling prophecy. If you expect bad things to happen, then your brain seeks out evidence of this to prove you right. As a result, you will be less likely to notice opportunities that are helpful to you, and will be primarily alert to the negative. If, on the other hand, you are an optimist, then your brain will seek out evidence to support that way of thinking. Opportunities will present themselves, and you will notice them and follow them up. The good news is that we are not destined to remain pessimists. With sufficient practice using NLP techniques, you can start the process of rewiring your brain. The brain is a muscle like any other in the body, and with repetition and persistency you can stop negative thoughts in their tracks and foster a spirit of positivity that is natural and useful to you.

When it comes to grief, NLP can be very effective in helping us to appreciate and understand that we have a right to a happy and fulfilled future, despite our tragic experiences. It does not mean that we pretend that everything is okay and adopt a 'Pollyanna' mentality, wandering around in total oblivion to the outside world. It does mean, however, that we can retain perspective, that we can realise that our loved ones want us to thrive, and that they would be terribly unhappy if we remained crippled by our grief to the extent that it was beginning to negatively affect our lives, relationships, careers, and businesses. It is understanding that we can continue to grieve for our loved ones whilst at the same time moving forward with our lives. Notice how I said 'moving forward' and not 'moving on'. There is a subtle but important difference. When we move forward, we do so in honour of those that are no longer with us, and we never forget them. They drive and inspire us to move forward and live our lives in a way that would make them even more proud of us than they already are.

Coaching

Following on from the death of my parents, I built upon my NLP studies by completing my coaching qualification. I became an accredited coach with the International Coaching Federation. Having informally been coaching my clients for the previous 25 years, I now had an official accreditation to recognise the specific coach relevant training that I had gone through. So, what is coaching, and how did it help me to navigate my grief journey?

For me, coaching is supporting a person to change and develop in a way that is consistent with their values and goals. Coaching also supports a person at every level on their journey to becoming who they really want to be. It also creates and develops awareness, empowers choice, and facilitates change.

It's not about telling people what to do. It is, instead, about asking questions that help a person to maximise their performance, and helps them to learn. The essence of coaching is to empower and enable a client to become the best version of themselves, by posing pertinent questions that inspire that person to arrive at their own conclusions and create their own solutions. As a direct result of this approach, the client is far more likely to achieve sustainable long-term success than had they simply been trained and told what to do.

As part of my coaching training, I was encouraged to develop and adopt a 'coach approach' to my life, both personally and professionally. A coach approach is all about asking questions, being curious about the answer, and perhaps not expecting an answer straight away, but being confident that the subconscious will seek out an answer over time and surprise us when we least expect it. It is this approach that helped me with my grief. I have been trained to seek out solutions to challenges, and it is an engrained way of thinking that I have forever. I have been coached to help myself achieve my personal best and to produce the results that I desire in my personal and professional lives. The net result of this approach is that I am abundantly aware of what I am capable of. Whilst in the depths of my grief, I would frequently remind myself of how resourceful I am, and sometimes this alone would make me feel better. On other occasions, I needed to go a bit further and ask myself some questions. Questions such as:

- What do I want?
- How do I want to feel right now?
- Am I getting a secondary gain from my grief? If so, what is it, and how can I achieve that from something other than grief?
- Do I believe that I need to suffer with grief in order to honour my love for Mum and Dad?

The beauty about questions like these are that we don't need the answers – or at least, not straightaway. We can trust that the answers will emerge and present themselves to us just when we need them to. By asking the questions early on, we give our subconscious mind time to process the questions and their content. Over time, neurological connections are made which create what I call 'Eureka moments'. This is when we have epiphanies, and these can be very helpful in terms of assisting us to gradually make sense of a situation which defies logic and probability. Coaching has helped me to trust that I can create a process I can follow that is going to put me in control of a specific situation. During a period of enduring circumstances that have been beyond my control, my coach approach has enabled me to identify the parts of my life that I do have control over, and to focus intensely on those. This then has the result of creating certainty in my life, which makes me feel safe and secure. I can then use this as a foundation upon which to grow. If I continue to ask more challenging questions, then having built up a degree of inner resilience my subconscious has a greater chance of helping me to find solutions to more taxing problems. The more I do this, the less significant are the elements that are beyond my control, until they become gradually less and less important to me.

Hypnotherapy

I achieved my accreditation as a Master Practitioner in Hypnotherapy in August of 2020, one month before I achieved my ICF Coaching accreditation. It is no coincidence that my determination and resolve to grow and develop as a person intensified whilst I was managing my grief. Interestingly, I started both my coaching and hypnotherapy journeys before Covid, and fulfilled them both during. For me, hypnotherapy was a natural progression following on from my NLP journey, and I had been privately intrigued by the power of hypnotherapy for many years. When I took my NLP Master Practitioner course in 2017, we were taught some basic principles of hypnotherapy, because much of NLP is inspired by the American psychiatrist and psychologist Milton Erickson. Erickson specialised in medical hypnosis, and he became the primary influence for the NLP community when it came to his approach to facilitating change and transformation whilst in trance.

So, in addition to Hypnotherapy being a natural progression from NLP, I also had an ulterior motive which I referenced in an earlier chapter. Before Mum died, she was in a lot of pain. She had a very high pain threshold, but even she struggled with the persistency of such acute pain as a result of her various arthritic and rheumatic conditions. I wanted to learn hypnotherapy so that I could help Mum to manage her pain, and also to help her manage her relationship with pain. Unfortunately, she died before I could complete the course and begin to help her in that way. I did, however, help her briefly on the day after her surgery in March 2020 – the last time that I saw her alive. Her surgery had been successful, and she had not at that stage contracted the virus. Despite the success of her surgery, she had been in a lot of natural and post-operative pain. I could see that she was in distress that day, so I began talking to her in gently rhythmic tones and meter. I encouraged her to notice the sound of my voice and the touch of my hand as I held hers in mine. I guided her to concentrate on her breathing, and gradually she appeared to settle down and become calm. I can still see Dad's face on the other side of Mum's bed, staring at me as I calmed her down, and I know that just listening to me calmed him, too. He had been fraught with worry, and felt helpless to assist his wife who was in so much pain. I will never forget this memory, which has had such a profound impact on me.

I could choose to be sad that Mum didn't survive to fully experience the extent of my support with hypnosis. Or I could choose to be proud that I offered her a special moment of peace in the days leading up to her death. I can also choose to be proud of the work that I have completed since my accreditation, helping our clients to facilitate change, whether that be for weight loss, anxiety management, or to build confidence. I know what Mum and Dad would be proud of, and that confirms my choice.

As you can see, my accreditation helped me from a symbolic value perspective, closely anchored to the memory of my parents. In fact, I dedicated my accreditation to the memory of Mum and Dad, which made me beam with pride. One of the best things about hypnotherapy is that you can use it on yourself, and I did use self-hypnosis to help me manage my grief. For those of you unfamiliar with hypnotherapy, the most helpful way to think about it is like a very intense form of meditation, where you experience a change midway through the process. You can learn how to do it yourself or you can hire a practitioner to do it for you. I found it so very helpful, as it kept me grounded and present when there was a lot of noise going on around me. I used it to help me feel at peace with the world and to block out all of the toxic chatter. I also used it to help myself become more tolerant and less angry, and to experience a sense of oneness with the universe. All of these outcomes helped me to manage my grief, and by tapping into my subconscious I could experience longer lasting change.

It's not a case of job done now – far from it. It's great, though, to understand that I have all of these amazing resources available to me whenever I need them. Again, sometimes just knowing that they are there is enough.

Conclusion

Concluding my story causes me to reflect upon the title of the book – Transforming Grief:From Tragedy Emerges Hope. So, let's break it down and address each part. Transforming Grief suggests that there is a porous nature to grief, that it can be perhaps manipulated. And I would agree with that. At no point did I reject my grief; in fact, I probably embraced it. Having embraced it, however, I transformed it into something that could simultaneously preserve the integrity of my love, honour, and respect for Mum and Dad, whilst also utilising its fuel to evaporate my fear and to ignite my passion. The journey that I speak of probably started many years ago when I embraced my personal development journey. It took a tragic set of events to accelerate the journey onto its ultimate trajectory, taking me from tragedy to hope. And in reality, that journey is still ongoing, and will be for the rest of my life. I can be grateful that I have learned so much about myself, others, and life in general, despite such an awful event acting as the catalyst.

My hope is that whatever challenges you face throughout your life, you give yourself permission to pause, reflect, and understand what each event means to you. I hope that you can learn to grow, learn to be brave, and learn to have compassion, as the healing process starts its long and winding journey.

You already have the resources that you require to navigate your way through tragedy – we all do! I simply urge you to give yourself a chance to demonstrate to yourself what you are capable of.

About the Author

Gavin Perrett is a multiple business owner, author, motivational speaker, and mindset transformation coach.

Gavin's roles in business and professional accreditations include:

www.liddleperrett.com – Co-founder

www.hawkhurstinvest.com – Co-founder, and Sales & Marketing Director

www.willprotect.co.uk – Co-founder, and Sales & Marketing Director

www.identityresource.co.uk – Co-founder, and Creative Director

Master Practitioner in Neurolinguistic Programming

Master Practitioner in Hypnotherapy

ICF Accredited Coach

Practitioner in Behavioural Change

Certificate in Applied Neuroscience

Advanced NLP Business Practitioner

Identity by Design – Licensed Trainer

Certificate in Core Transformation

Resources

The most wonderful aspect of personal development is sharing knowledge and experiences with others to enrich their lives as well as your own. With this in mind, I am thrilled to share the following online resources which can act as a gateway for those of you who are keen to find out more about how to enjoy a similar growth journey to mine.

https://www.achieveyourgreatness.co.uk/

https://itsnlp.com/

https://ginagardiner.com/index

https://identityresource.co.uk/

http://robertdilts.com/

https://anlp.org/

https://coachingfederation.org/

9 781839 757914